First Published in Australia 2026 by Tracey Jones Photography
Address: 56 Alchera Drive, Mossman, QLD, 4873
Email: info@traceyjonesphotography.com
Phone: 0497 055 151
Website: www.traceyjonesphotography.com

Written by © Tracey Jones Photography

Images, diagrams and photographs by © Tracey Jones Photography

ISBN: 978-1-7640796-4-8 (paperback); 978-1-7640796-5-5 (e-book)

Table of Contents

Introduction

This book is designed to help you understand exposure in a clear, practical, and approachable way.

It is written for photographers using DSLR or mirrorless cameras that allow control over shutter speed, aperture, ISO, and camera modes. If your camera has modes such as Manual, Aperture Priority, or Shutter Priority, this book is for you.

Rather than focusing on memorising settings, this book aims to help you understand how exposure works, why settings affect your images, and how to make confident decisions when photographing different scenes.

How to Use This Book

This is a hands-on book and works best when used actively rather than read once and put away.

You can use it in a couple of different ways:
- You may choose to read through the theory first, then work through the practical exercises at the end.
- Or you may prefer to move through the book section by section, revisiting the exercises as you complete each part.

While both approaches work, the book is designed to be read in order, as each chapter builds on the previous one. Concepts introduced early on are used later, particularly in the practical exercises.

Learning at Your Own Pace

You don't need to understand everything immediately.

Exposure is one of those topics that often becomes clearer with time and practice. It's completely normal to read something once, try it in the real world, and then come back to the explanation again later with fresh understanding.

This book encourages that process. You're not expected to rush — or to get it perfect.

A Practical Focus

Throughout the book, the emphasis is on:
- Understanding what your settings are doing
- Learning how different choices affect your images
- Building confidence through observation and practice

By the time you reach the exercises at the end, you'll have the tools you need to start applying what you've learned in a way that feels manageable and practical.

This book is designed to be returned to, marked up, and used alongside your camera. Take your time with it, experiment often, and allow your understanding of exposure to grow naturally as you practise.

What is Exposure?

Photography is the act of capturing light.

Every photograph you take is created using light — whether that's bright sunlight, soft window light, or the last glow of the day as the sun sets. Exposure is the term we use to describe how much of that light your camera captures.

If your photo looks too bright, it has captured too much light.
If your photo looks too dark, it hasn't captured enough light.

Understanding exposure is one of the most important steps in learning photography, because exposure affects every image you take, no matter what you are photographing.

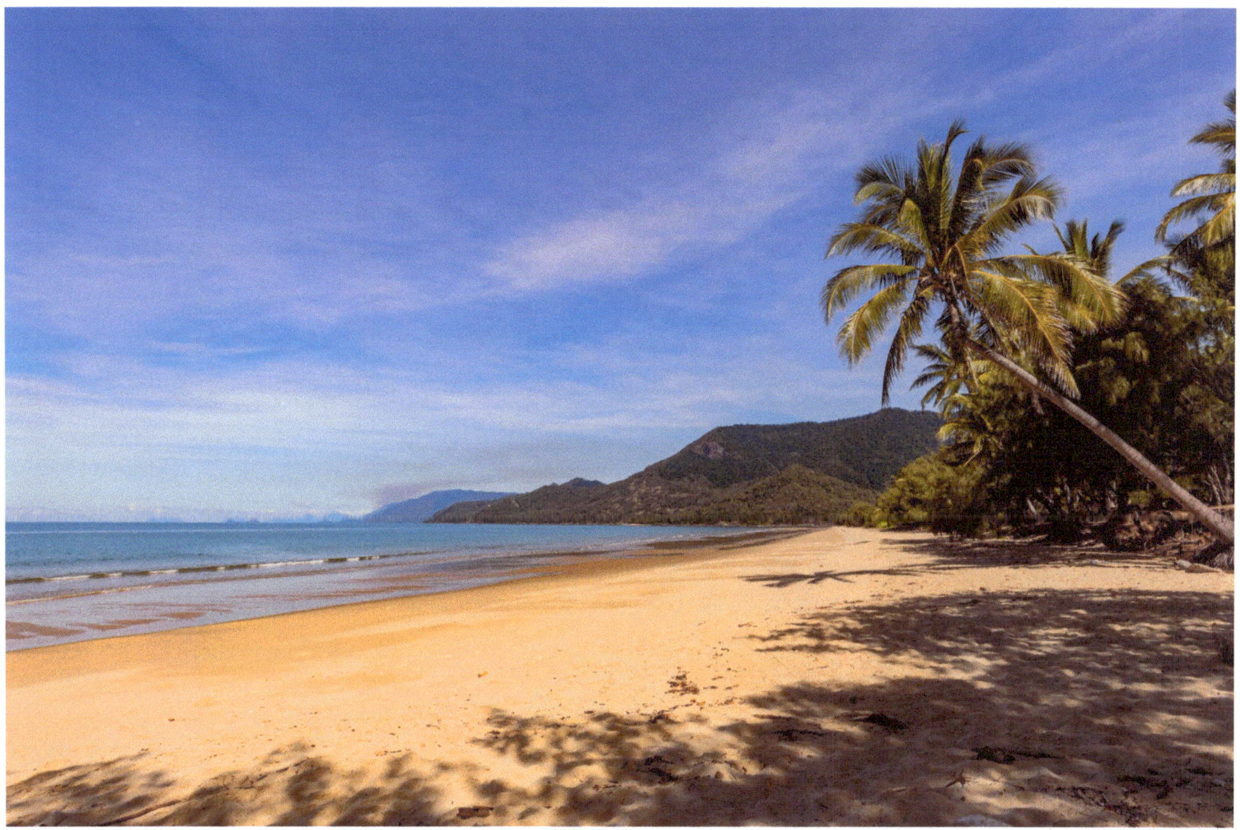

The exposure in this image is well balanced, allowing detail to be seen in both the shadows and the white clouds.

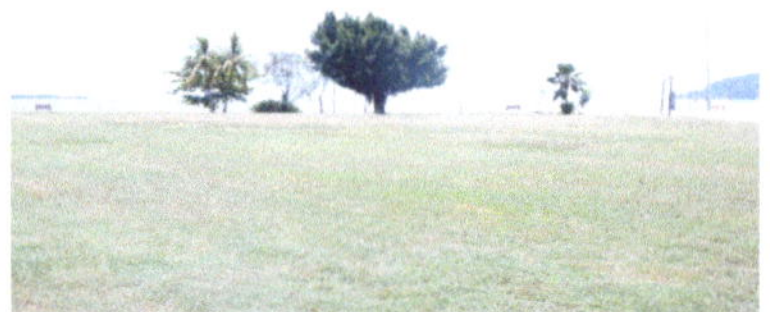

Very Overexposed

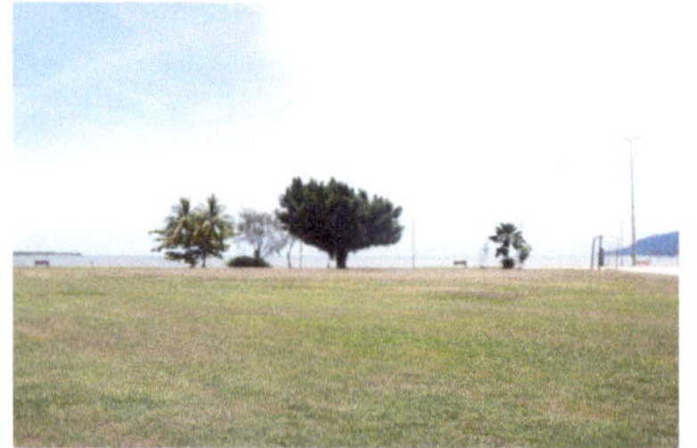

Overexposed

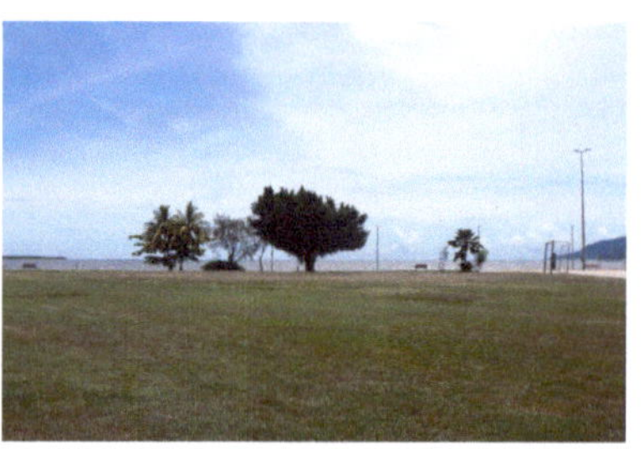

Correct exposure

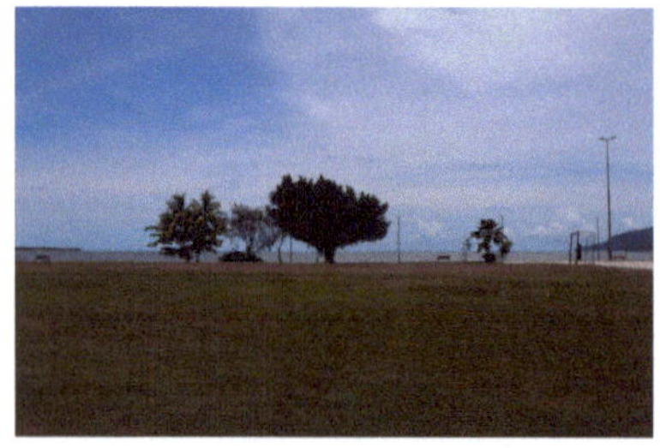

Underexposed

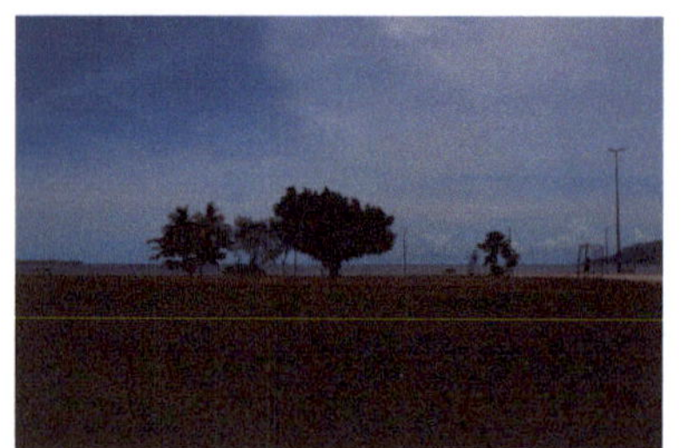

Very Underexposed

What Does "Correct Exposure" Mean?

A correct exposure is when your image has captured enough light to clearly show the subject and the details you want the viewer to see — not too bright and not too dark.

However, photography is a creative art form, and exposure is not always about getting everything perfectly balanced. What looks correct to one person may look slightly too bright or too dark to someone else.

This means that exposure is not about rigid rules. It is about understanding how light behaves and how your camera responds to it, so you can make deliberate choices rather than relying on guesswork.

Too Bright vs Too Dark

When an image is overexposed, too much light has been captured.

Bright areas can lose detail, colours may appear washed out, and highlights may turn pure white.

When an image is underexposed, not enough light has been captured.

 Shadow areas can lose detail, parts of the image may appear black, and the subject can become difficult to see.

Learning to recognise these differences is an important part of developing your eye as a photographer. As you work through this book, you'll learn how to adjust your camera settings to correct these issues and take control of your exposure.

Why Exposure Changes So Quickly

One of the most challenging parts of exposure is that light is constantly changing.

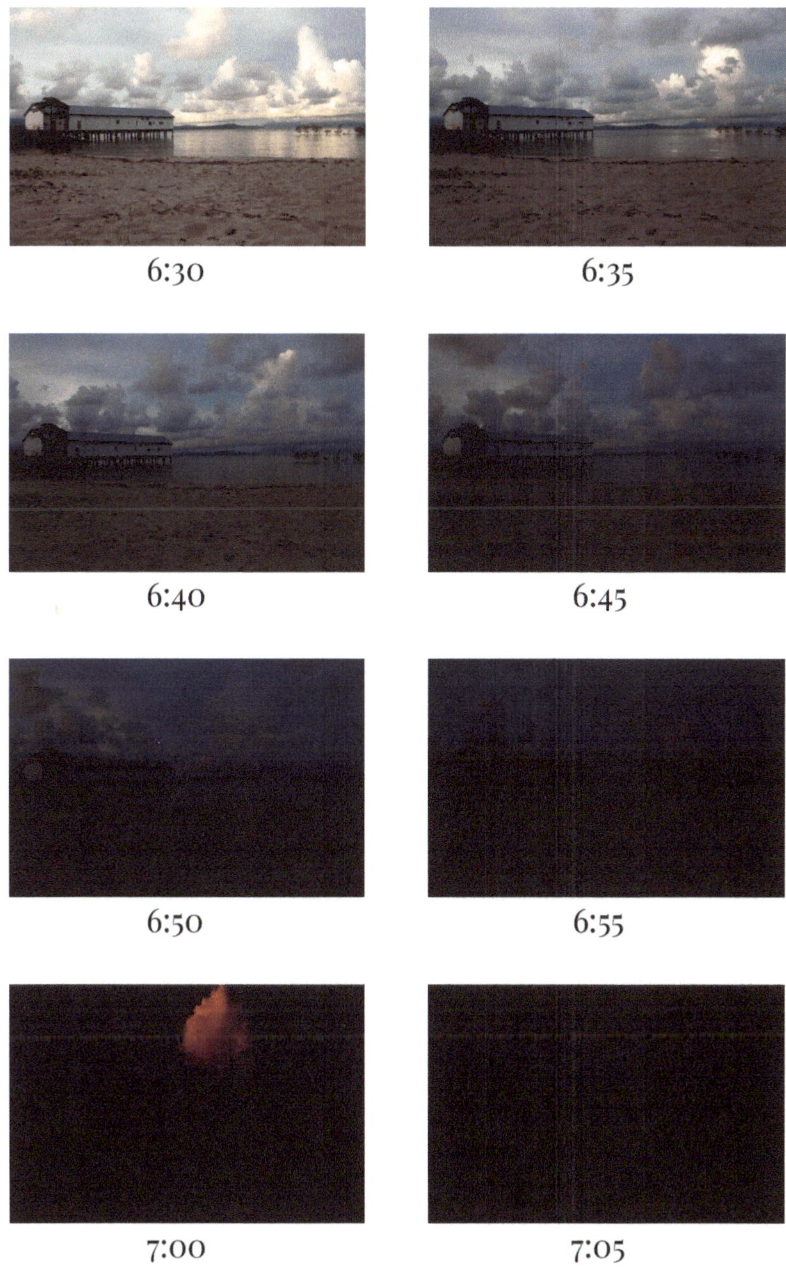

6:30

6:35

6:40

6:45

6:50

6:55

7:00

7:05

Even if your subject stays exactly the same, the available light can change:

- As clouds move across the sun
- As the sun gets lower in the sky
- As you step into shade or back into light
- As you slightly change your shooting angle

Sometimes this change happens over minutes — and sometimes it happens in seconds.

This means the camera settings that worked a moment ago may no longer give you the same result. Exposure is not something you set once and forget. It requires you to continually observe the light and adjust your settings as conditions change.

This is especially noticeable during sunrise and sunset, when light levels can change dramatically from one shot to the next.

In this series of images, the first image taken at 6:30 pm was a correct exposure. The following images were taken using exactly the same settings to show how quickly light changes as the sun sets.

How Your Camera Controls Exposure

Your camera controls exposure using three main settings:
- Shutter Speed – how long the camera's shutter stays open to capture light
- Aperture – how wide the lens opening is and how much light it lets in
- ISO – how sensitive the camera's sensor is to light

These three settings work together to control how bright or dark your image appears. This relationship is known as the Exposure Triangle.

Each setting affects exposure in a different way, and each one also influences how your image looks creatively. Understanding how they work together is the key to moving beyond Auto mode and taking control of your camera.

Understanding Exposure Stops

Exposure is measured in "stops." A stop is simply a way of describing a doubling or halving of the amount of light entering the camera. If you increase your exposure by one stop, you double the light. If you decrease it by one stop, you halve the light. Shutter speed, aperture and ISO can all be adjusted in stops, which makes it easier to balance them when using the exposure triangle.

On most modern cameras, settings are adjusted in smaller steps called third stops. This means that instead of changing a full stop at a time, the camera allows you to make smaller, more precise adjustments. Three of these smaller steps equals one full stop. The overall principle remains the same — a full stop still represents a doubling or halving of light.

Throughout this book, whenever settings are adjusted or compared, the changes refer to these standard stop values, whether full stops or smaller increments.

Understanding what exposure is lays the foundation for everything that follows. In the next chapter, we'll look at the Exposure Triangle as a whole before exploring each setting in detail.

The Exposure Triangle

In the previous chapter, we looked at what exposure is and why it matters. Now it's time to look at how your camera controls exposure.

Your camera does this using three main settings:

- Shutter Speed
- Aperture
- ISO

These three settings work together to control how bright or dark your photo appears. This relationship is known as the Exposure Triangle.

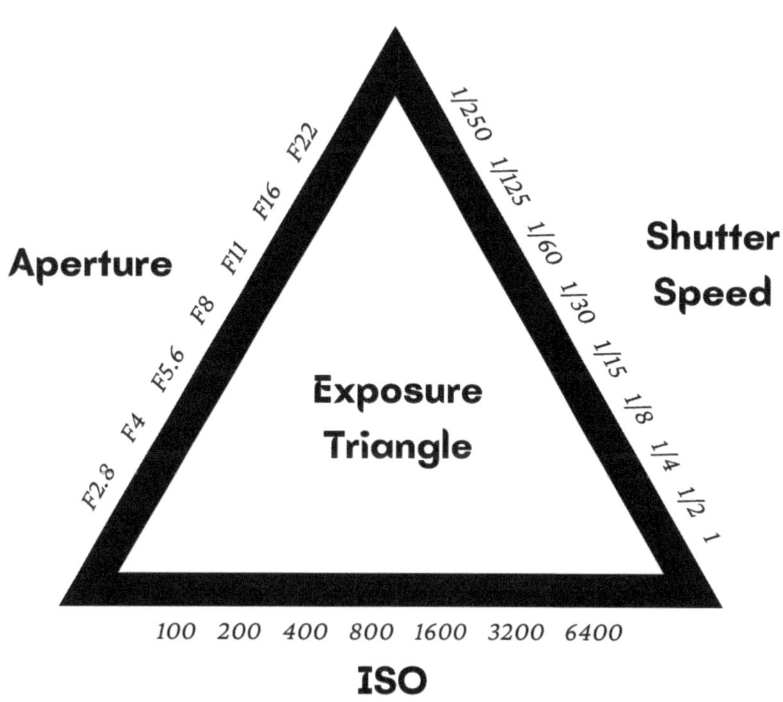

The Three Parts of the Exposure Triangle

Each side of the Exposure Triangle plays a different role.

Shutter speed controls time, aperture controls the size of the lens opening, and ISO controls sensitivity to light. When combined, these three settings allow you to balance brightness while shaping how your final image looks.

Although these settings all affect brightness, they also affect your photos in different creative ways. Because of this, exposure is not just about getting the image bright enough — it's also about deciding which setting matters most for the photo you want to take.

How the Exposure Triangle Works

The key thing to understand about the Exposure Triangle is that the three settings are linked. If you change one side of the triangle, at least one of the other sides must also change to keep the exposure balanced.

For example:
- If you let in more light by changing the aperture, you may need to reduce how long shutter is open.
- If you allow light to enter the camera for longer using a slower shutter speed, you may need to reduce the amount of light entering the camera by using a smaller aperture.
- If you increase the camera's sensitivity to light using ISO, you may need to reduce the amount of light that enters the camera by using a slower shutter speed or smaller aperture.

These adjustments work together to control the overall brightness of your image. This is why exposure can sometimes feel like a balancing act.

Each of these changes is measured in stops. If you increase one setting by one stop (doubling the light), you will need to decrease another setting by one stop (halving the light) to maintain the same overall exposure.

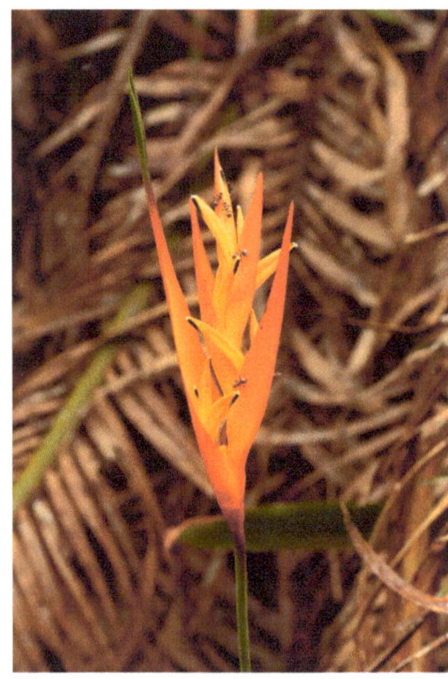

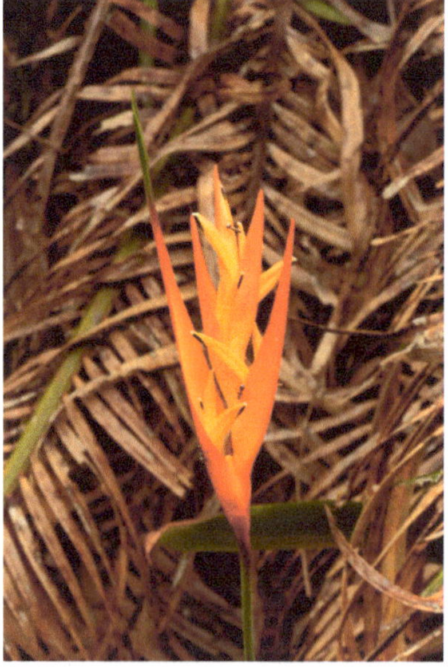

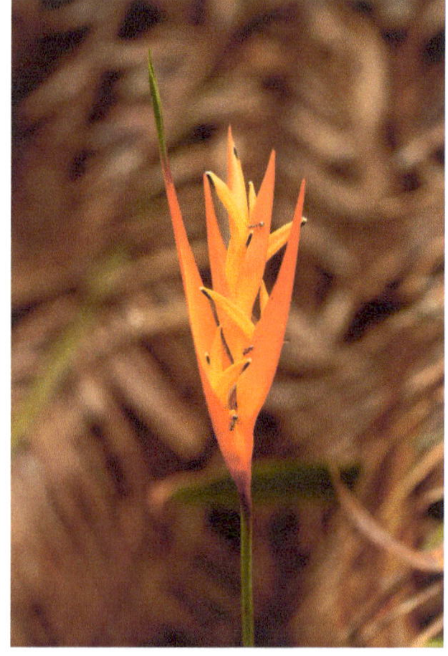

Fast shutter speed, medium aperture, high ISO.

Slow shutter speed, small aperture, medium ISO.

Fast shutter speed, big aperture, medium ISO.

Trade-Offs and Compromises

Each setting comes with its own side effects:
- Shutter Speed affects motion blur and camera shake
- Aperture affects depth of field and background blur
- ISO affects image quality and noise

This means there is rarely one "correct" combination of settings. Instead, there are often several different ways to achieve a similar exposure — each with a different look or feel.

Understanding these trade-offs is what allows you to move from letting the camera decide, to making deliberate creative choices.

You Don't Adjust All Three at Once

A common mistake beginners make is trying to change all three settings at the same time.

In practice, most photographers:
- Decide which setting is most important for the scene
- Set that first
- Adjust the other settings to balance the exposure

The image to the right was taken in a very dark room, so I used a high ISO, which has left some noise in the darker parts of the image.

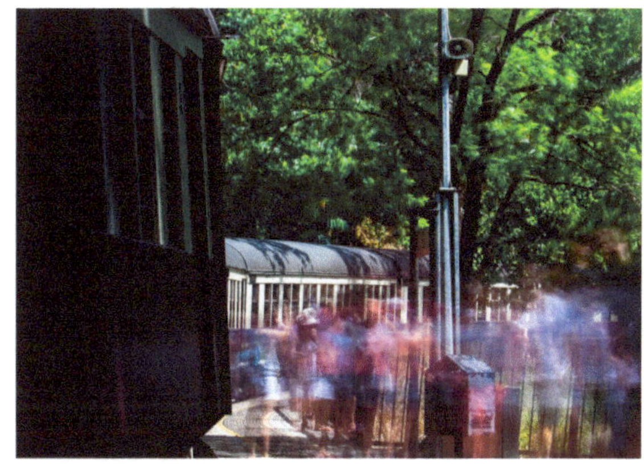

In the image above, using a long shutter speed created motion blur amongst the people moving along the train platform.

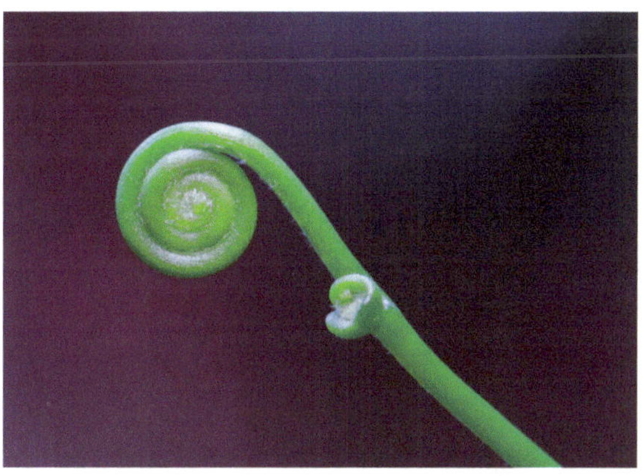

In the image above, using a large aperture created a blurry background.

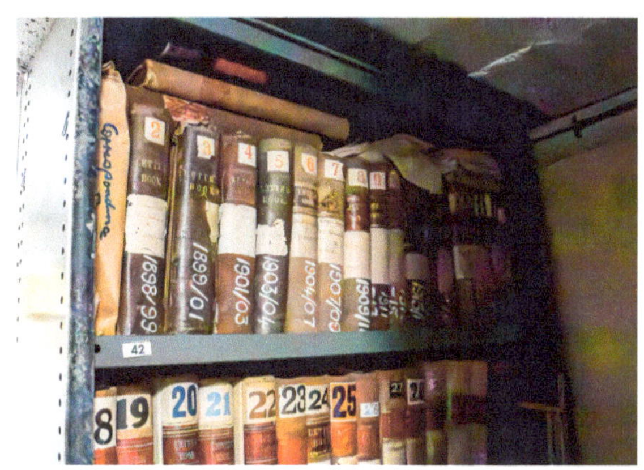

For example:

- If your subject is moving, shutter speed is usually the priority
- If you want a blurred or sharp background, aperture is usually the priority
- If you're shooting in low light, ISO may need to increase

We'll explore this decision-making process in much more detail later in the book.

The Exposure Triangle Is a Tool, Not a Rule

It's important to remember that the Exposure Triangle is a way of understanding exposure, not a strict set of rules.

It helps explain:

- Why changing one setting affects the others
- Why your camera behaves the way it does
- Why two photos can look very different even if they are the same brightness

Once you understand the Exposure Triangle, exposure starts to feel far less mysterious — and much easier to control.

In the next few chapters, we'll break the Exposure Triangle down and look at each setting individually, starting with Shutter Speed.

By the end of these chapters, you'll understand:

- What each setting does
- When to prioritise one over another
- How to combine them confidently

Shutter Speed

Inside your camera is a small shutter that opens and closes each time you take a photo. Shutter speed refers to how long that shutter stays open, allowing light to reach the camera's sensor.

The longer the shutter stays open, the more light is recorded.
The less time it stays open, the less light is recorded.

Shutter speed is measured in seconds or fractions of a second, such as 1 second, 1/60, or 1/1000. Changing from 1/125 to 1/250 reduces the light by one stop, meaning the image becomes half as bright.

Shutter Speed and Brightness

Shutter speed directly affects how bright or dark your image appears.

- A longer shutter speed lets light in for a longer period of time, resulting in a brighter image
- A faster shutter speed lets light in for a shorter period of time, resulting in a darker image

If you photograph the same scene using different shutter speeds, the brightness of the image will change, even though the light and other settings stay the same.

This is one of the ways shutter speed contributes to exposure, but brightness is only part of the story.

Images to the right; Same scene photographed at different shutter speeds

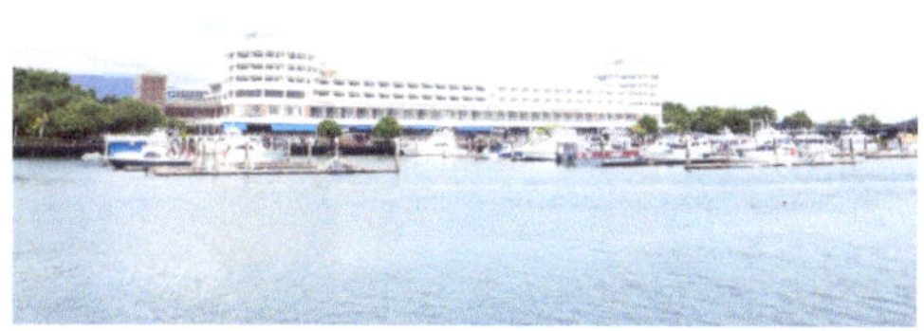

1/25

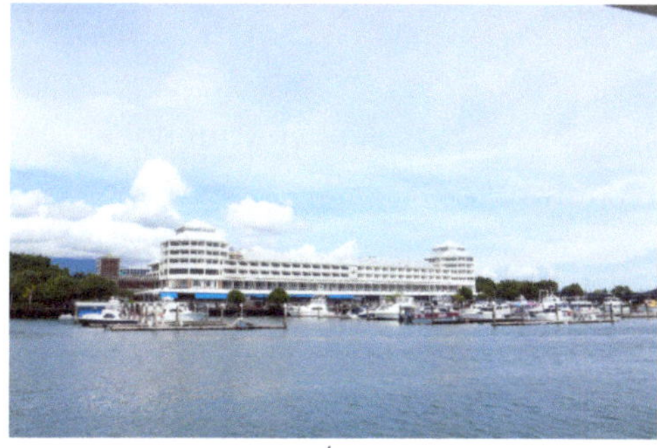

1/50

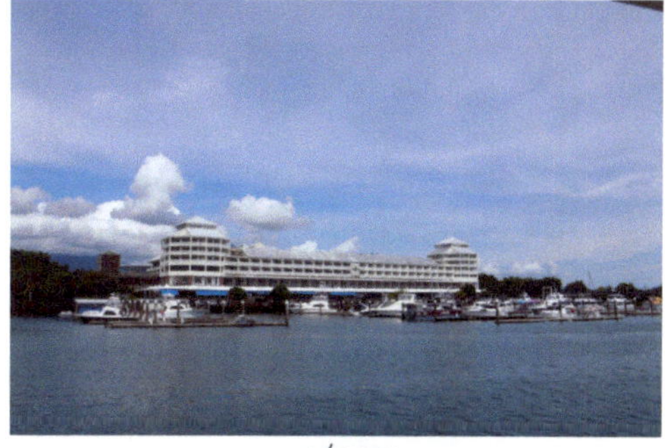

1/100

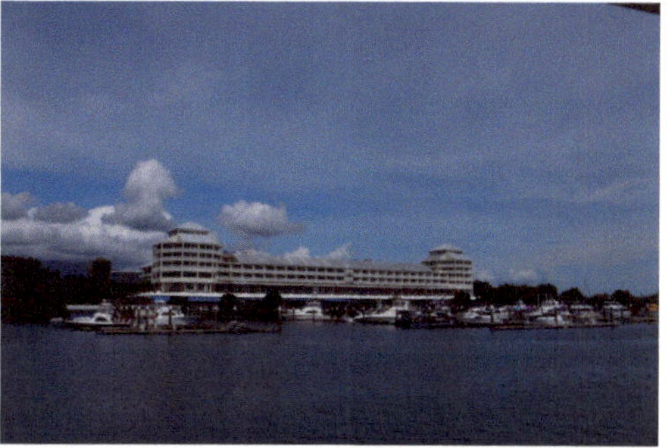

1/200

Shutter Speed and Motion

Because shutter speed controls time, it also controls how movement appears in your photos.

When the shutter opens, the camera begins recording light. If your subject moves while the shutter is open, that movement will also be recorded in the image. The longer the shutter remains open, the more movement is captured.

A fast shutter speed allows the camera to capture a very short moment in time. Because the shutter is only open briefly, there is little opportunity for movement to be recorded.

A slow shutter speed keeps the shutter open for longer. During this time, any movement that occurs will be recorded, resulting in motion blur.

Because of this, fast shutter speeds freeze movement, while slower shutter speeds allow motion to blur.

This applies whether the movement comes from your subject or from the camera itself.

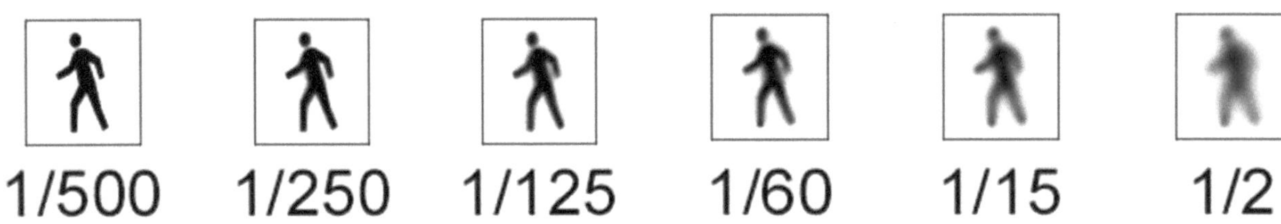

The diagram above shows a person walking across the frame.

At a slow shutter speed, the camera records the person's movement as they walk, resulting in a blurred figure.

As the shutter speed becomes faster, less of that movement is recorded. The person appears progressively sharper because the camera is capturing a shorter moment in time.

This same principle applies to all moving subjects — from people and animals to cars and flowing water.

The images below show the same scene photographed at different shutter speeds. Slower shutter speeds record the movement of the water as blur, while faster shutter speeds freeze that movement.
The subject and lighting remain the same — changing the shutter speed alone changes how movement is captured.

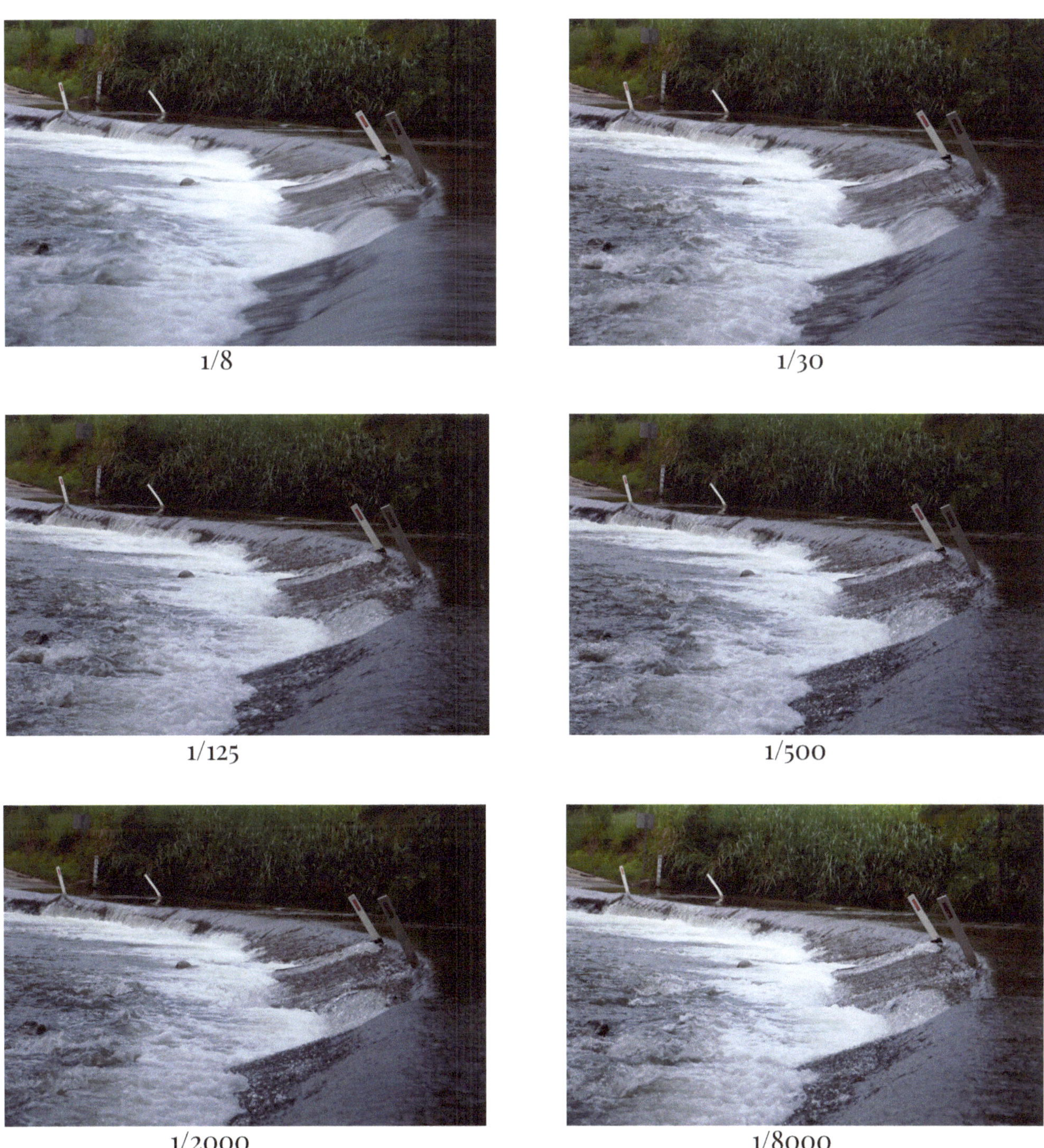

1/8

1/30

1/125

1/500

1/2000

1/8000

Creative Use of Shutter Speed

Shutter speed isn't just a technical setting — it's a creative tool. Motion blur is not always a mistake. In many cases, it is used creatively to show movement, direction, or the passage of time.

For example:
- A slow shutter speed can create a smooth, silky effect in flowing water
- A fast shutter speed can freeze a split second of action, such as splashing water or flying birds
- A slow shutter speed can be used to create light trails or to paint with light, recording the movement of light sources over time

In all cases, the subject is the same — the difference is how time is recorded.

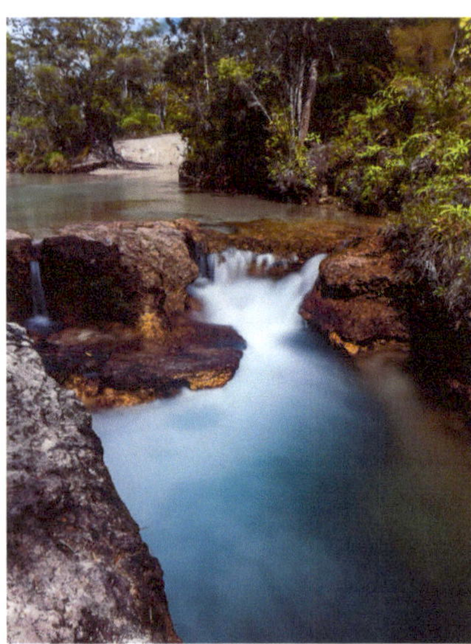 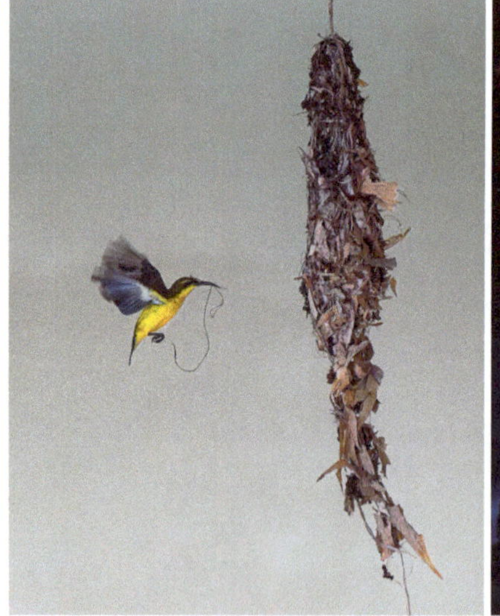 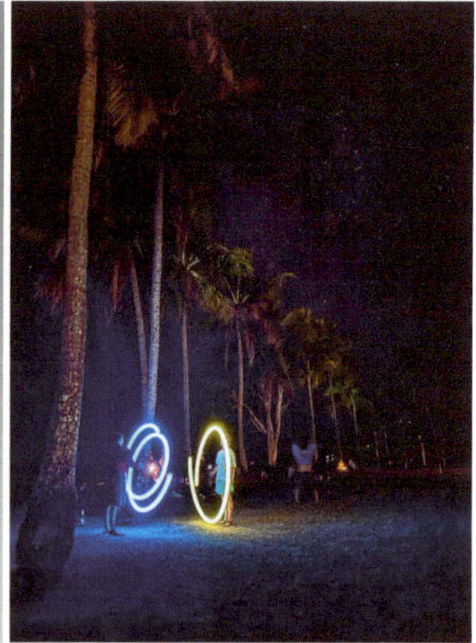

30 seconds; A long shutter speed was used to record the movement of the water over time, creating a smooth, silky, mystical effect as it flows over the rocks.

1/1000 second; A fast shutter speed freezes the sunbird mid-flight as she builds her nest, with slight blur still visible in the wings due to their rapid movement.

1 second; A one-second exposure captures the full circular motion of the light poi, turning movement into a visible trail of light within the scene.

Camera Shake and Hand-Holding

Motion blur doesn't only come from moving subjects. It can also come from camera shake. When you hand-hold a camera, it is very difficult to keep it completely still. Even small movements — such as pressing the shutter button — can cause blur if the shutter speed is too slow.

As a general guideline:
- Most people can hand-hold a camera safely at around 1/60 of a second
- Slower shutter speeds increase the chance of camera shake

If you are using a shutter speed slower than this, it's a good idea to:
- Use a tripod
- Use a remote release or self-timer
- Brace yourself against something solid

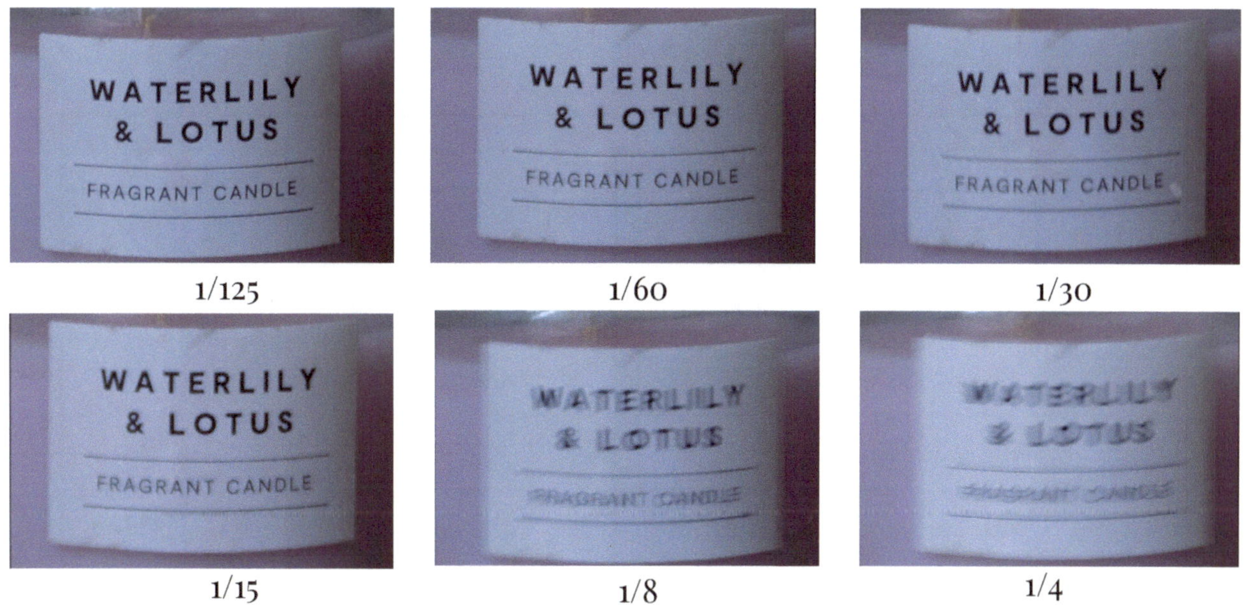

These hand-held images show how camera shake becomes more visible as shutter speed slows.
Each image is a zoomed-in section of the original photo, focusing on the text on the candle label so that changes in sharpness are easier to see.
At faster shutter speeds the text is sharp and readable, but as the shutter speed slows, blur becomes more noticeable — first in the smaller text and along the edges, and eventually across the entire label.

Lens Choice and Camera Shake

The type of lens you are using also affects how noticeable camera shake will be.

- Wide-angle lenses are more forgiving and show less shake
- Zoom or telephoto lenses magnify movement and show camera shake more easily

When using longer focal lengths, you will usually need a faster shutter speed to keep your images sharp, or extra support such as a tripod.

Choosing a Shutter Speed

There is no single correct shutter speed for every situation. The right shutter speed depends on:

- How fast your subject is moving
- Whether you are hand-holding or using support
- The look you want in the final image

The examples below are starting points, not rules. They are here to give you a sense of what different shutter speeds are commonly used for.

Fast athletes	1/4000	Landscapes (windy day)	1/125
Birds in flight	1/2000	Still Life	1/60
Moving Cars	1/1000	Panning	1/60
Aerial	1/1000	Landscapes (still day)	1/30
Slower athletes	1/500	Sunset	1sec
Wildlife	1/500	City lights at night	8sec
Children Playing	1/500	Low light indoors without flash	10sec
A person walking	1/250	Silky Water	15sec
Flowers	1/250	Light Painting	20sec
Portraits	1/250	Milky Way	30sec
Flash Photography	1/125	Star Trails	5min

What to Notice in Your Own Photos

When reviewing your images, ask yourself:
- Is the blur coming from the subject or the camera?
- Does the amount of blur match the look I wanted?
- Would a faster or slower shutter speed improve the result?

Being able to answer these questions will help you choose the right shutter speed more confidently.

What to Take Away from This Chapter

- Shutter speed controls how long light enters the camera
- It affects both brightness and motion
- Faster shutter speeds freeze movement
- Slower shutter speeds record movement and increase the risk of blur
- Shutter speed is often the first setting to consider when something is moving
- Understanding where the movement is coming from helps you decide whether you need a faster shutter speed, more support, or a creative approach.

In the next chapter, we'll look at Aperture, which controls how much light passes through the lens and how much of the scene appears in focus.

Aperture

Inside your lens is an adjustable opening made up of a series of overlapping blades. Aperture refers to how wide or narrow this opening is when you take a photo.

The size of this opening controls how much light enters the camera.
- A wide aperture lets in more light
- A small aperture lets in less light

Aperture is measured using F-numbers (also called F-stops), such as F2.8, F5.6, or F16. The smaller the F-number, the wider the opening inside the lens. This can feel confusing at first, because a low number actually means a larger opening that lets in more light.

Each full step between F-numbers changes the exposure by one stop. For example, moving from F4 to F5.6 reduces the amount of light entering the camera by one stop.

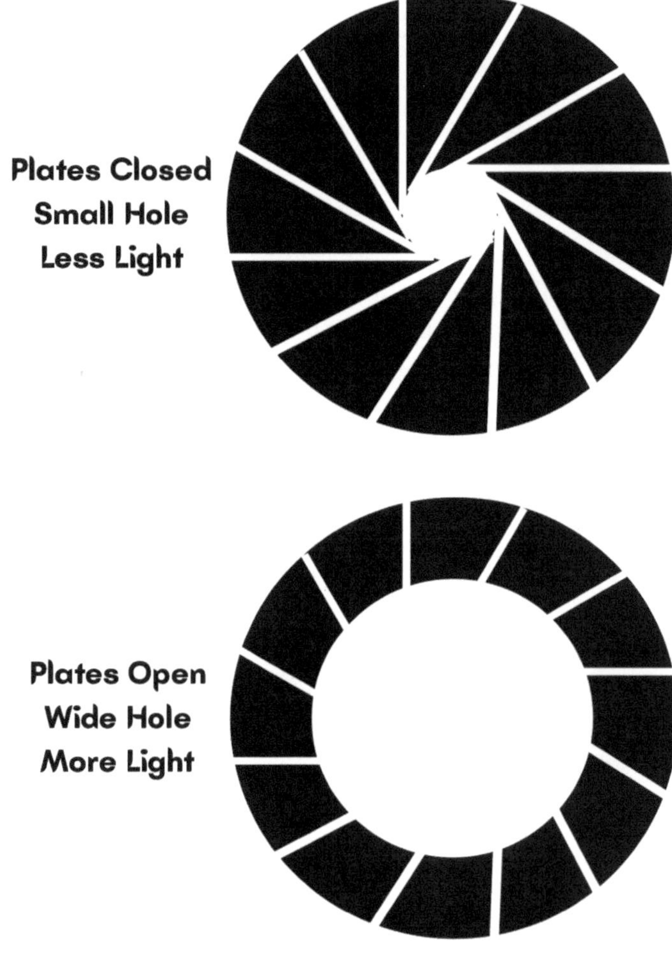

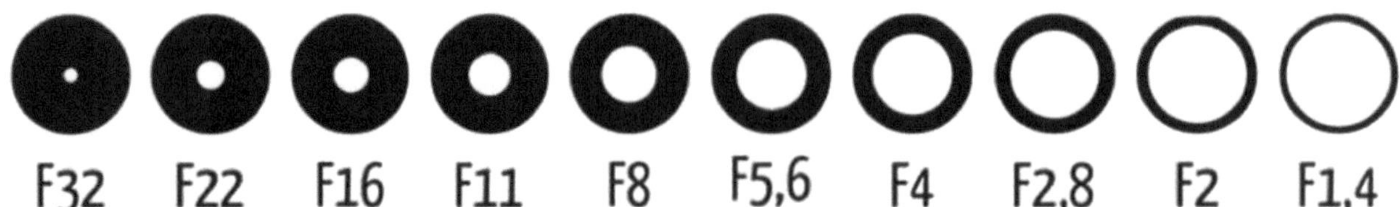

Aperture and Brightness

Aperture affects exposure by controlling the amount of light entering the camera.

- A wide aperture (small F-number) allows a lot of light in and produces a brighter image
- A small aperture (large F-number) restricts light and produces a darker image

If you photograph the same scene and only change the aperture, the brightness will change, even though the scene and lighting stay the same.

At this point, aperture behaves very similarly to shutter speed — but aperture has an additional effect that makes it one of the most important creative tools in photography.

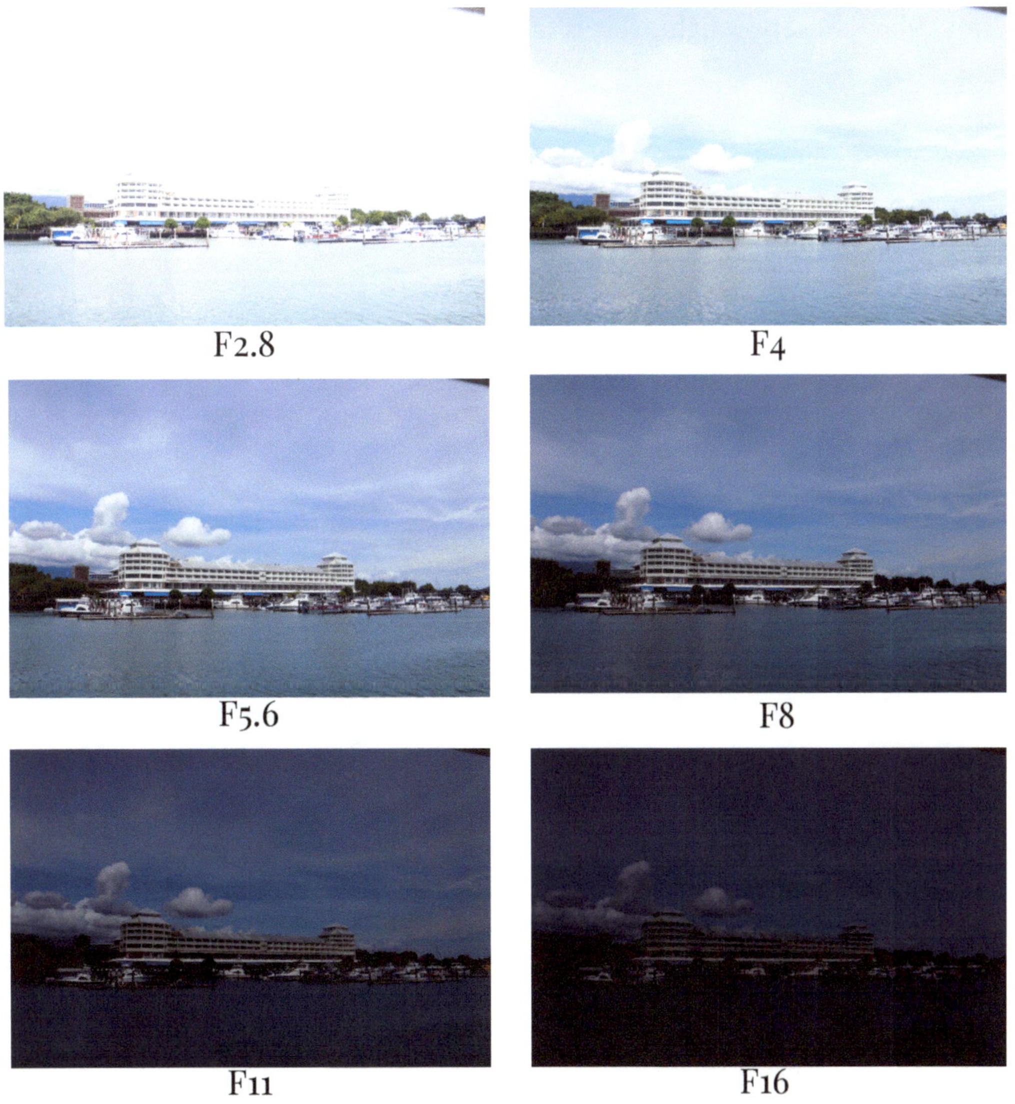

F2.8   F4

F5.6   F8

F11   F16

Aperture and Depth of Field

In addition to brightness, aperture also affects depth of field.

Depth of field refers to how much of the image appears in focus, from front to back.
- A wide aperture (low F-number) creates a shallow depth of field, where only a small part of the image is sharp
- A small aperture (high F-number) creates a large depth of field, where more of the scene appears in focus

This is why aperture plays such a big role in the look and feel of a photograph.

The diagrams below show how light travels through the lens and how that affects what appears in focus.

When the aperture is wide, light enters the lens at steeper angles. This results in a shorter zone of focus, meaning areas in front of and behind the focus point quickly fall out of focus and appear blury.

When the aperture is small, light enters at narrower angles. This creates a larger zone of focus, allowing more of the scene to remain sharp.

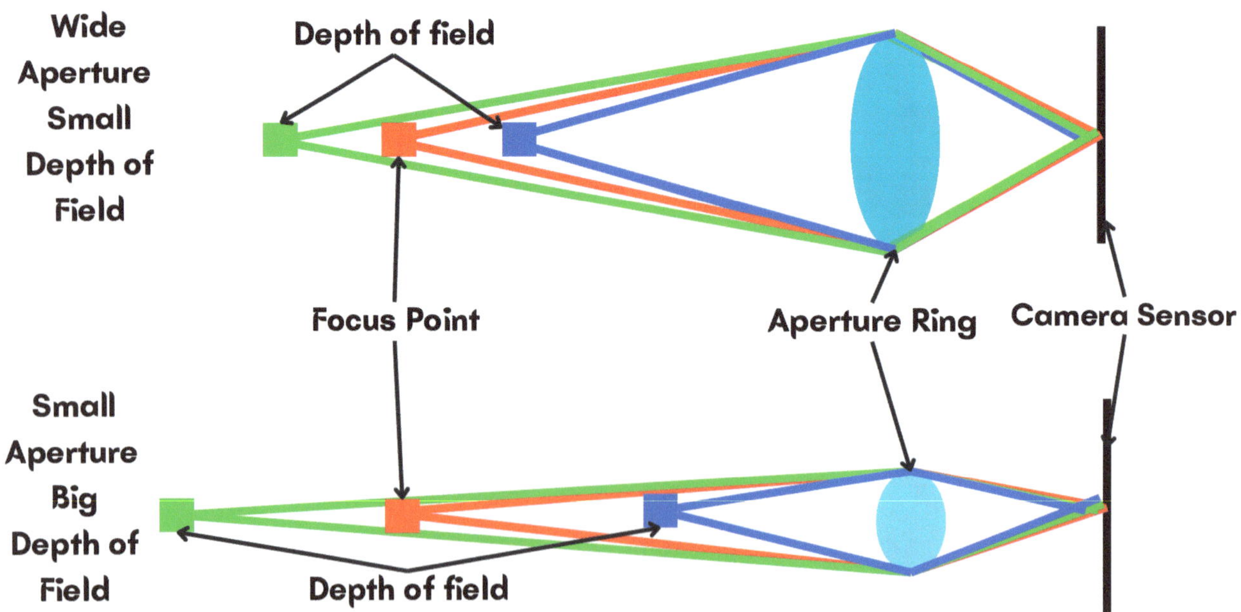

In these photos you can see that a wide aperture (low F-number) restricts the focal area (smaller depth of field) meaning that you can only read 1 or 2 of the numbers on the ruler.

A small aperture (high F-number) allows for more of the image to be in focus (greater depth of field) and you can read most of the numbers on the ruler,

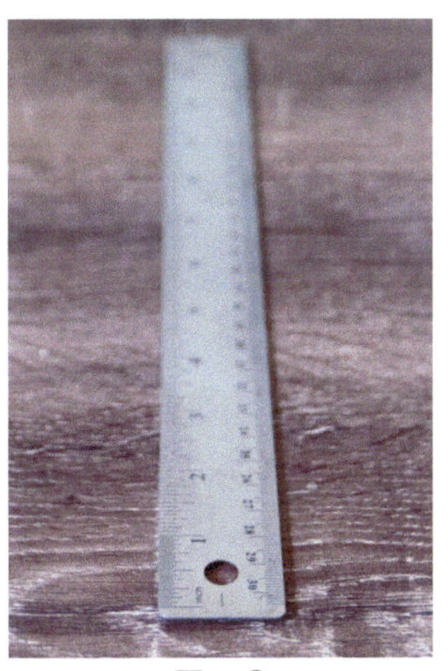

F2.8

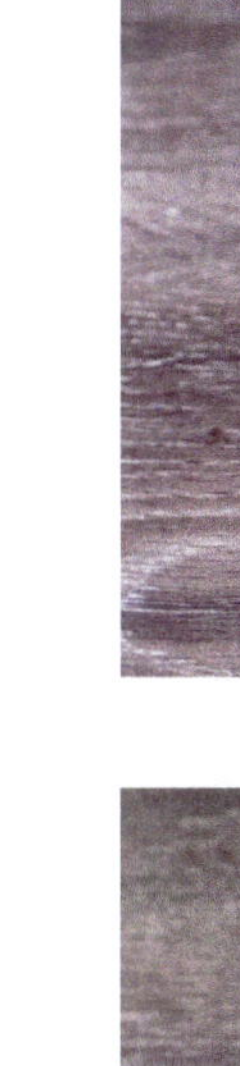

F4

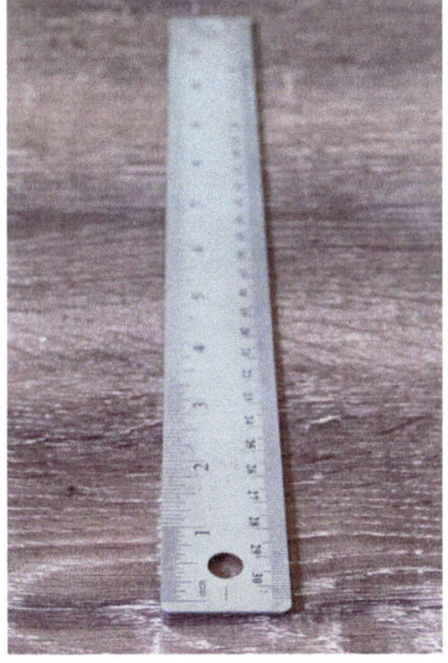

F5.6

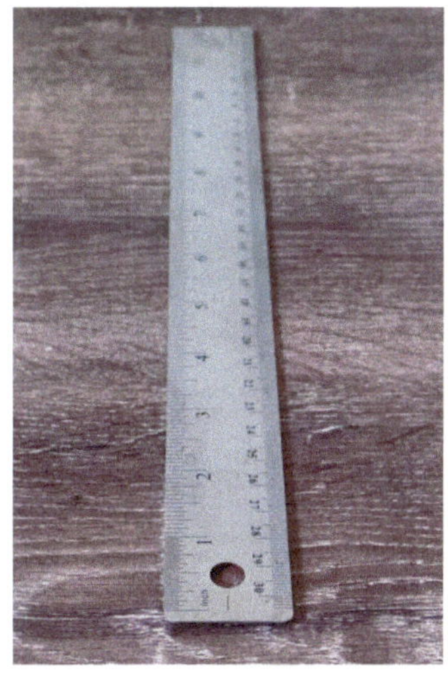

F8

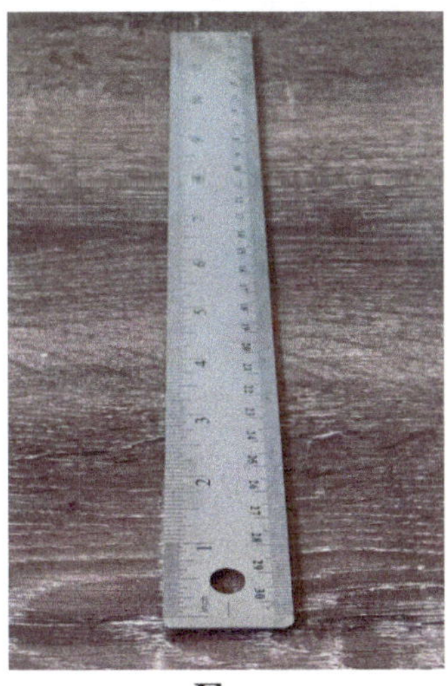

F11

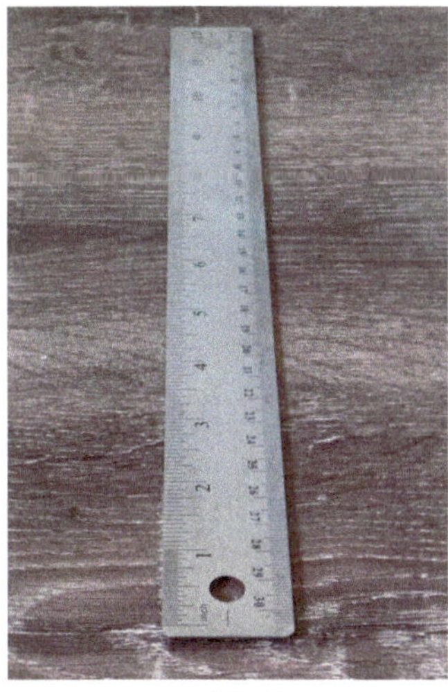

F16

Aperture in Real Photos

When looking at real photographs:
- Portraits often use wide apertures to blur the background and separate the subject
- Landscapes often use small apertures to keep the foreground and background sharp

F5.6

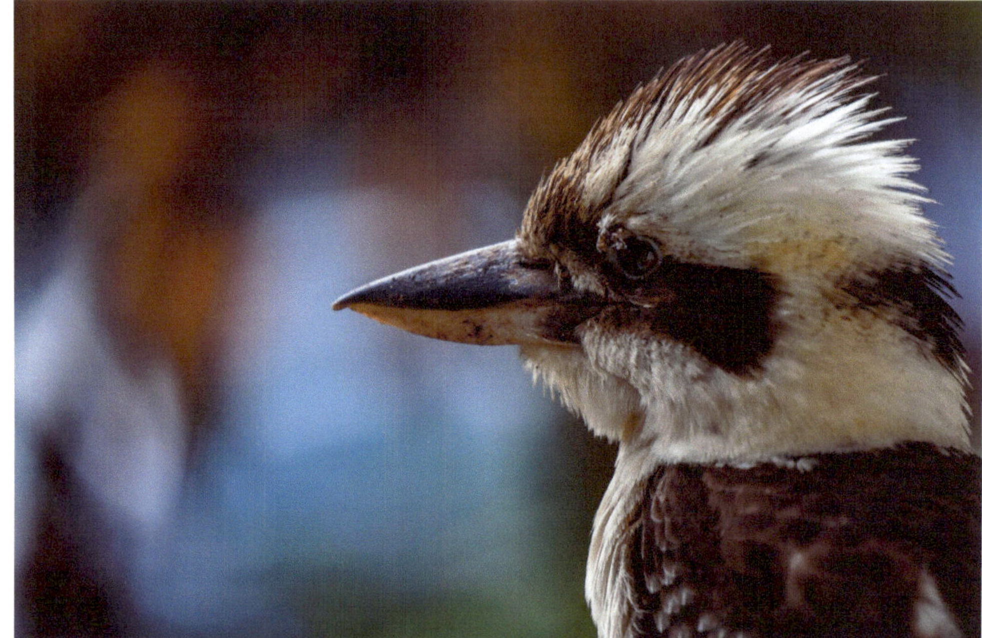

F16

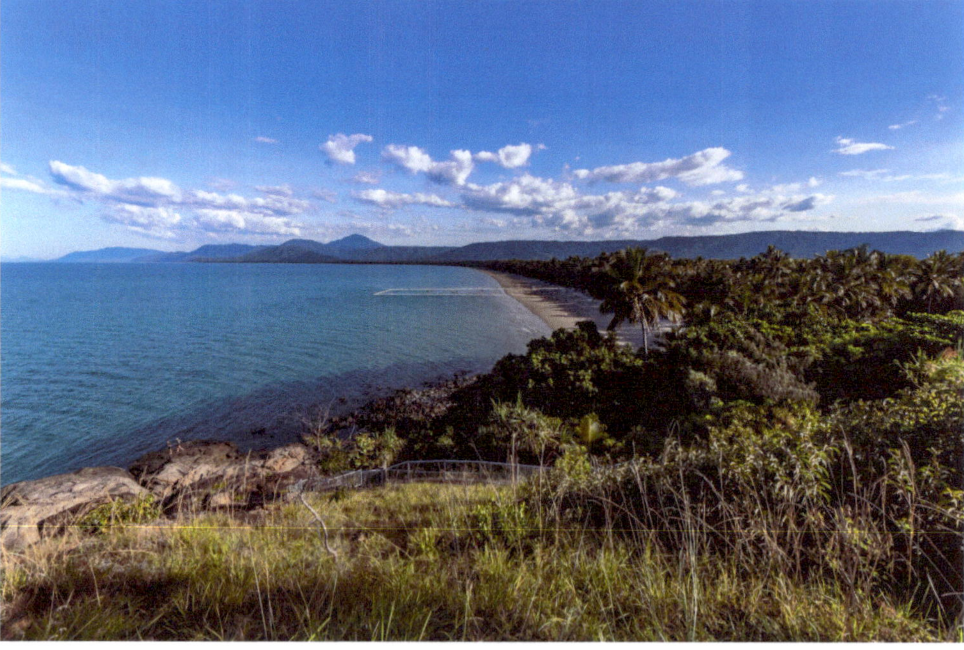

Focus Distance and Depth of Field

Depth of field is also affected by how close you are to your subject.

- The closer you focus, the smaller the depth of field becomes
- The further away you focus, the larger the depth of field becomes

This means that even if your aperture stays the same, depth of field can still change depending on where you focus.

This is especially noticeable when photographing small objects or details at close range.

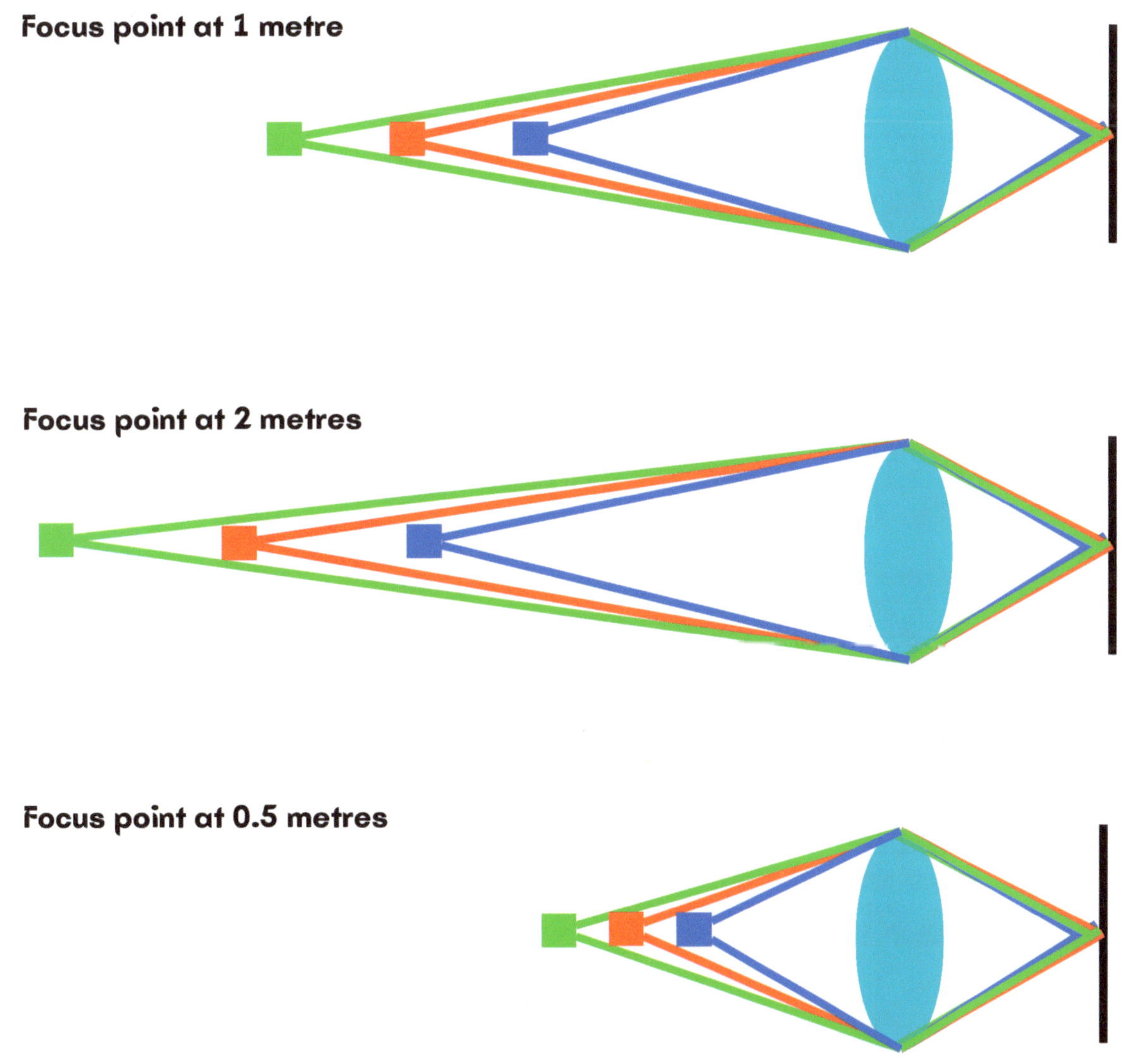

For these photos I have not changed the F-number but have moved the camera closer to the subject. You can see how as the camera gets closer to the subject the depth of field gets smaller. In each image the focus point is on the middle candle.

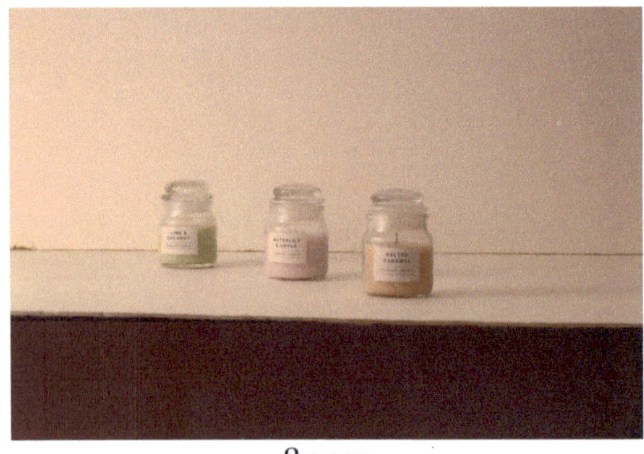

80cm

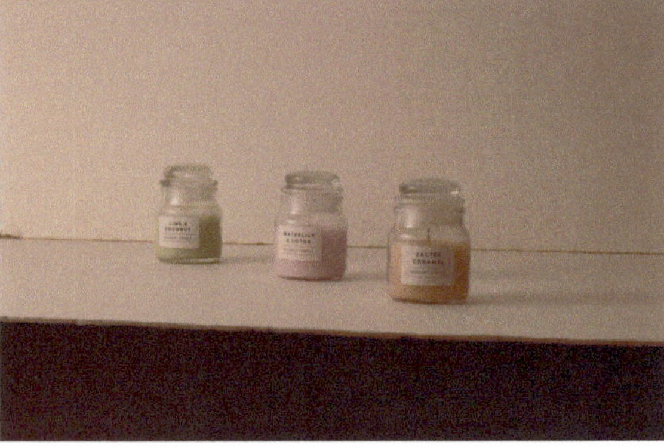

70cm

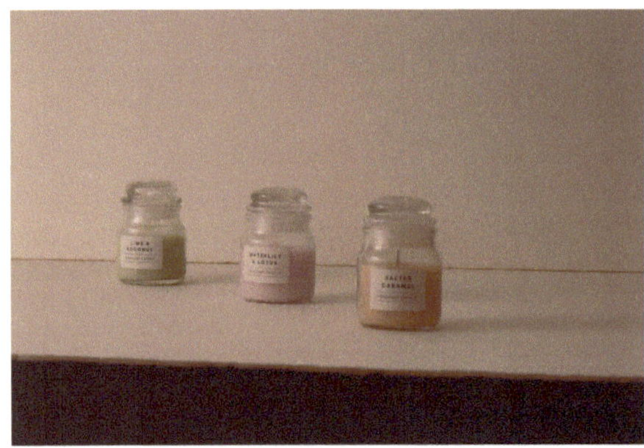

60cm

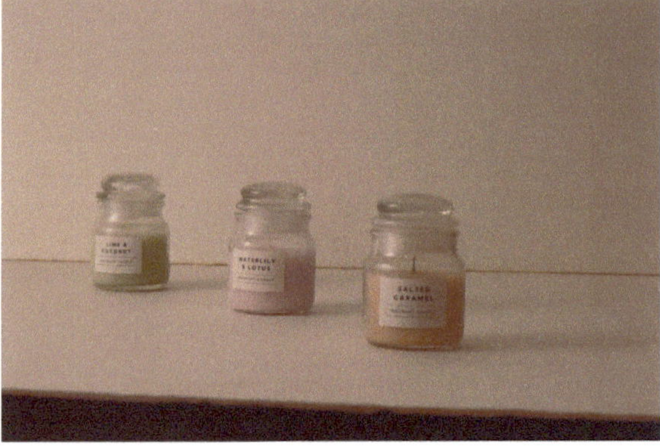

50cm

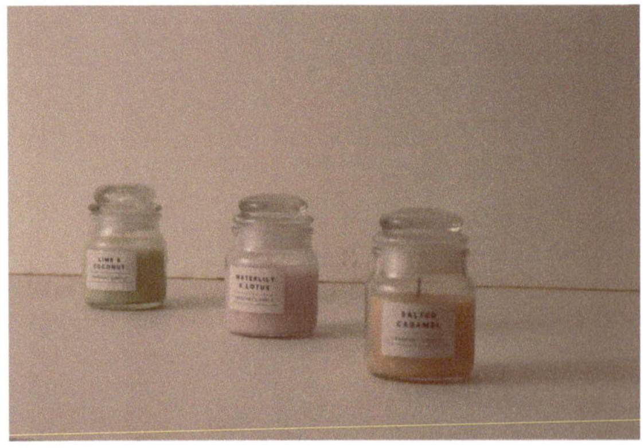

40cm

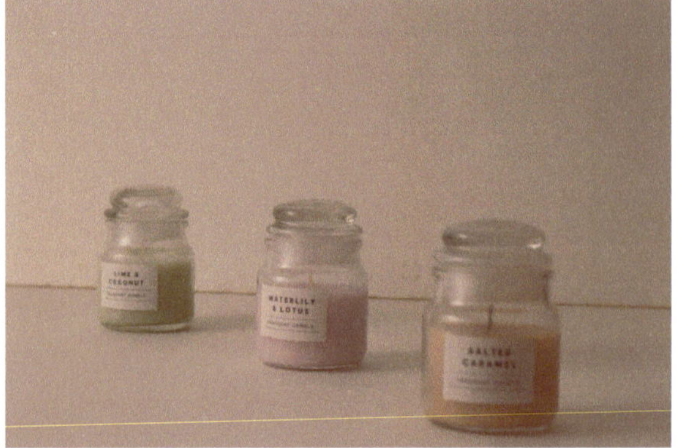

30cm

Focal Length and Depth of Field

The focal length of your lens also influences depth of field.

- Longer focal lengths (zoomed in) produce a shallower depth of field
- Shorter focal lengths (zoomed out) produce a larger depth of field

This is why backgrounds often appear more blurred when using telephoto lenses, even if the aperture number hasn't changed.

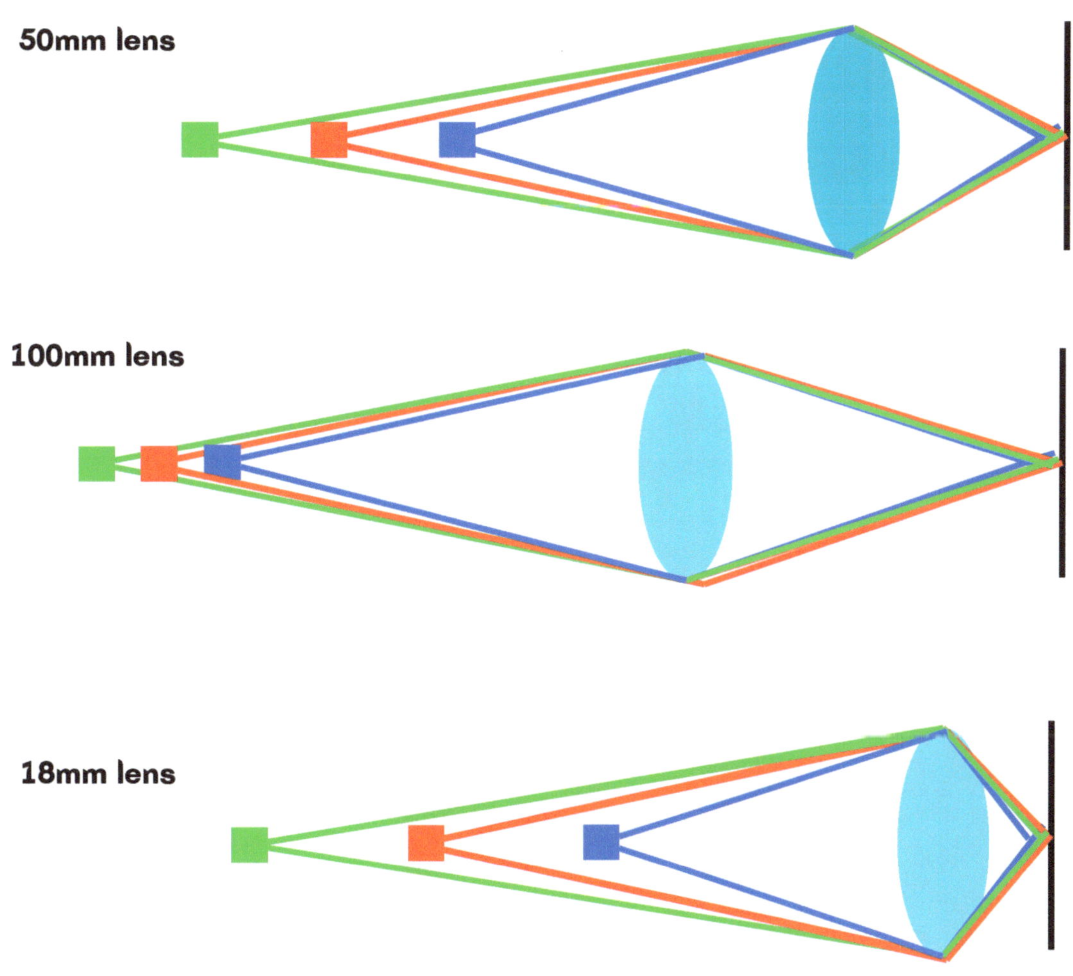

For these photos the F-number has stayed the same, but the focal length of the lens has changed. You can see how as I use a longer focal length the depth of field gets smaller. Again in each image the focus point is on the middle candle.

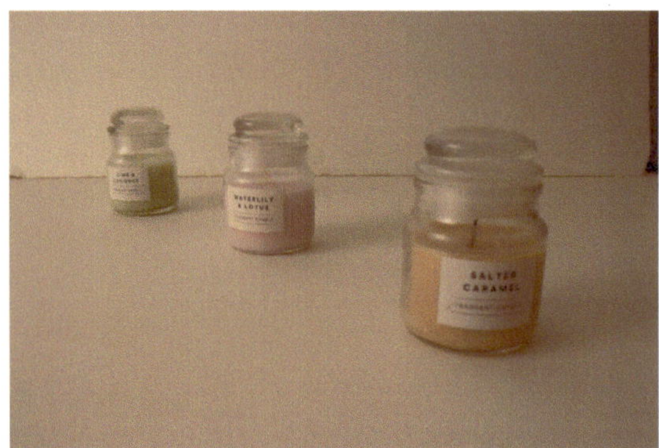

18mm

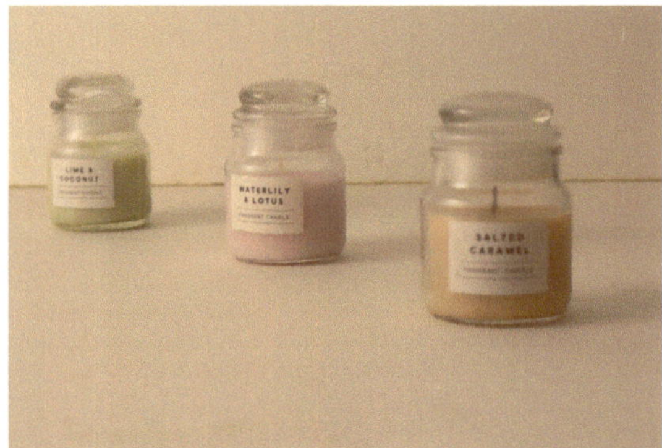

50mm

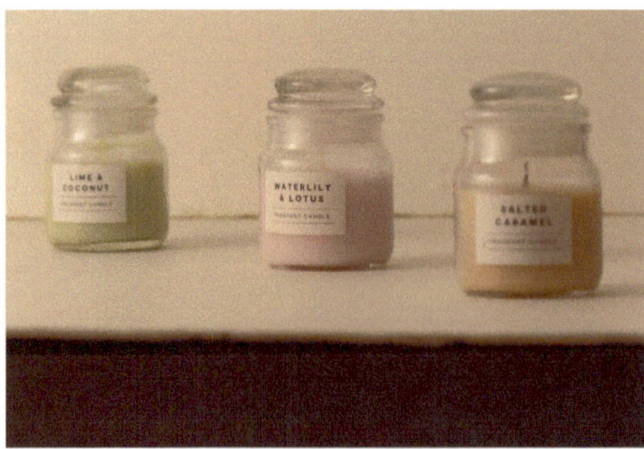

100mm

Choosing an Aperture

There is no single correct aperture for every situation. The aperture you choose depends on:

- How much of the scene you want in focus
- How much light is available
- The look you want to achieve

In practice, aperture is often the priority setting when depth of field matters most.

What to Take Away from This Chapter

- Aperture controls how much light enters the camera
- Wide apertuers let in more light
- It also controls depth of field
- Wide apertures blur backgrounds and isolate subjects
- Small apertures keep more of the scene in focus
- Aperture is a key creative tool, not just an exposure setting

In the next chapter, we'll look at ISO, which controls how sensitive your camera is to light and how that affects image quality.

ISO

Sensitivity and Image Quality

ISO controls how sensitive your camera's sensor is to light.

Unlike shutter speed and aperture, ISO does not control how light enters the camera. Instead, it controls how strongly the camera reacts to the light that is already there.

- A low ISO makes the camera less sensitive to light
- A high ISO makes the camera more sensitive to light

ISO values are shown as numbers such as ISO 100, 400, 1600, or 6400. Doubling the ISO increases exposure by one stop.

100 → 200 → 400 → 800 → 1600 → 3200 → 6400 → 12800 → 25600 → 40000

Less Sensitive	**More Sensitive**
Darker	**Brighter**

ISO and Brightness

ISO affects exposure by changing how bright or dark your image appears.

- A low ISO produces a darker image
- A high ISO produces a brighter image

If you photograph the same scene using the same shutter speed and aperture, but change only the ISO, the brightness of the image will change.

ISO is often used when there isn't enough light to achieve a correct exposure using shutter speed and aperture alone.

Increasing ISO does not add more light to a scene. Instead, it increases how strongly the camera responds to the light that is already there. This is why ISO can be adjusted quickly when light levels change, even if shutter speed and aperture remain the same.

These photos were taken one after the other, so there was very little change in available light. The only difference between these images is the ISO number. As you can see, the lower the ISO number the darker the image is, and the higher the ISO number the brighter the image is.

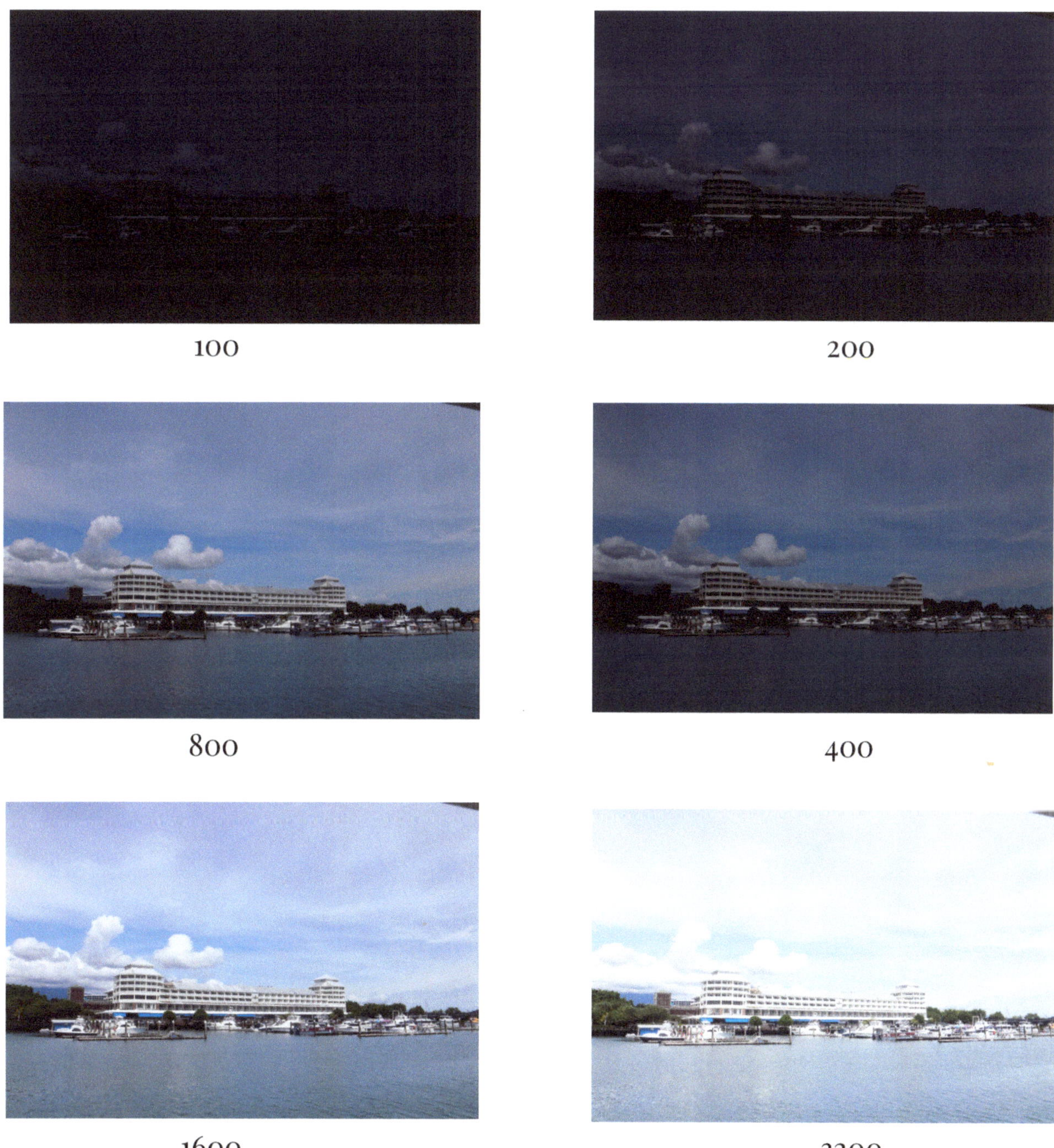

Understanding ISO Through Film (Why It Still Matters)

ISO comes from film photography.

In film cameras, film was made up of light-sensitive grains.
- Low ISO film had smaller grains and produced finer detail
- High ISO film had larger grains that reacted faster to light

Those larger grains were more visible in the final image.

Although digital cameras no longer use film, the term ISO is still used to describe how sensitive the sensor is to light.

ISO and Noise

As ISO increases, image noise becomes more visible.

Noise appears as small speckles or grain in an image and is most noticeable:
- In darker areas
- In shadows
- In low-light scenes

Noise does not usually appear evenly across the image. Areas with less light tend to show noise first.

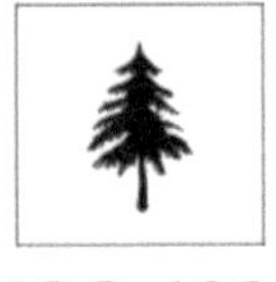

ISO 100

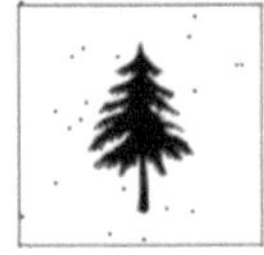

ISO 200

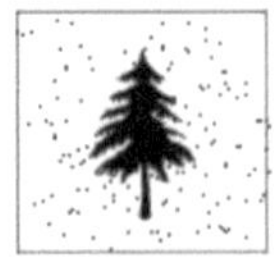

ISO 400

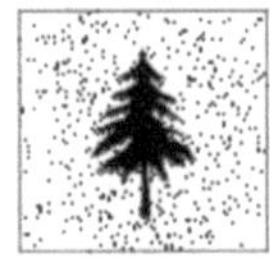

ISO 800

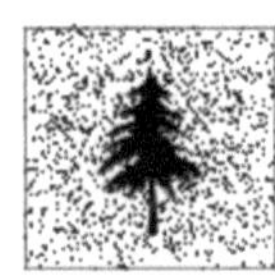

ISO 1600

Low ISO
Less Sensitive
Less Noise

High ISO
More Sensitive
More Noise

Noise is more noticeable in darker areas of an image. These 6 images were taken at night in a dark room. You can see that as the ISO increases, the image turns from black to a more red colour. This red colour is the noise.

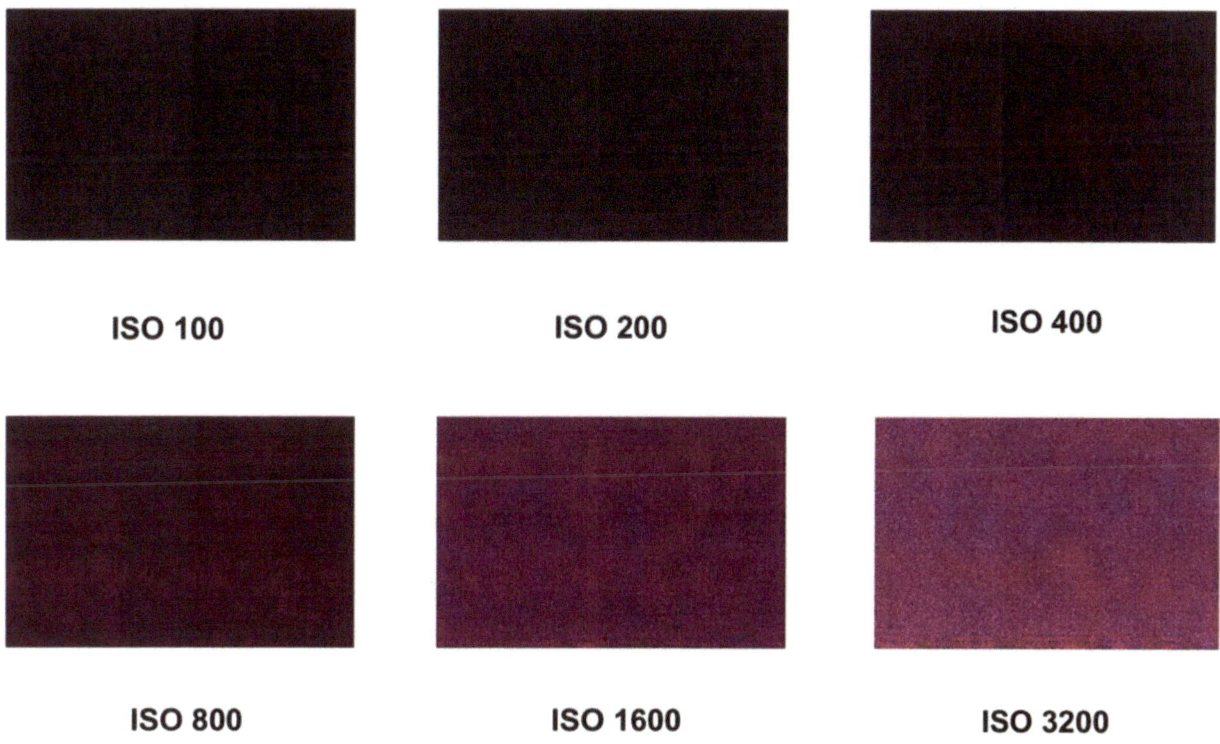

Digital Sensors and Modern Cameras

In digital cameras, the physical size of the sensor does not change when you increase ISO. Instead, the camera amplifies the signal coming from the sensor.

As this signal is amplified, noise becomes more visible.

Modern cameras handle noise far better than older cameras, and many can produce very usable images at high ISO values. Noise reduction software can also help reduce the appearance of noise during editing.

Because of this, ISO is often the least worrying side effect of the Exposure Triangle.

Here are some more examples of a dark subject on a dark background. When you zoom in you can really see the noise.

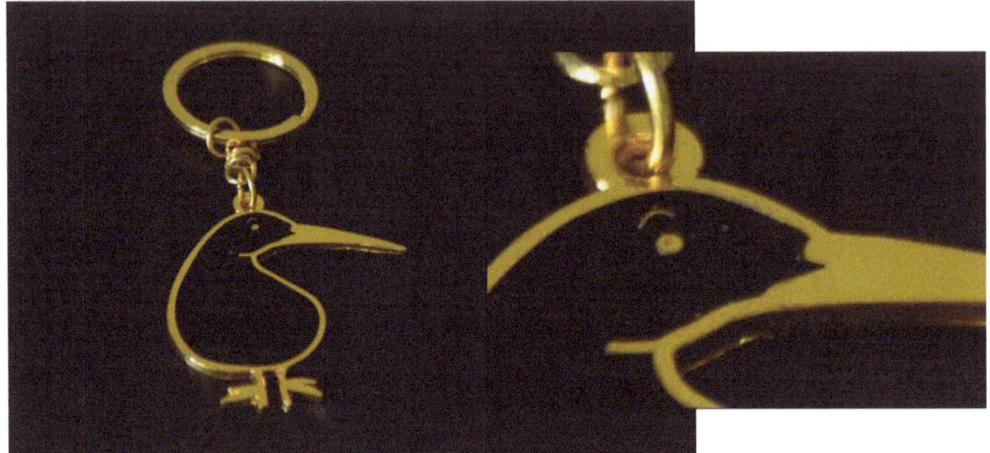

100

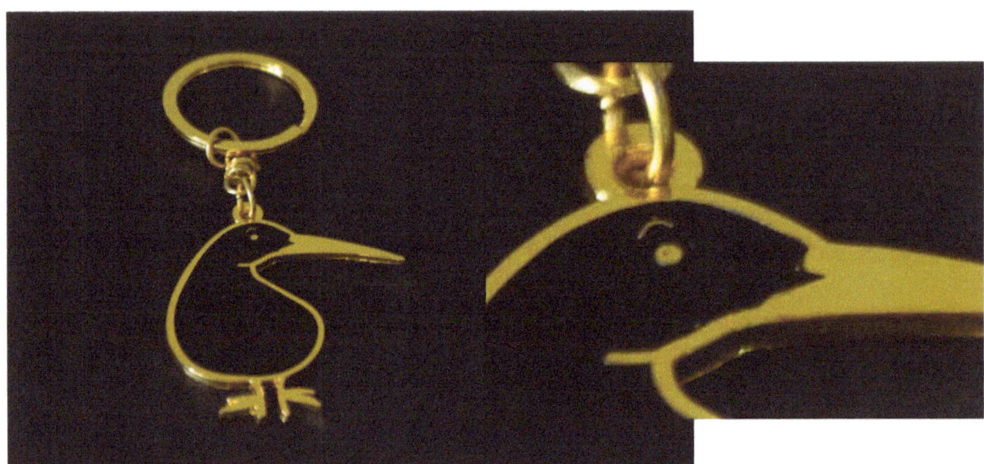

400

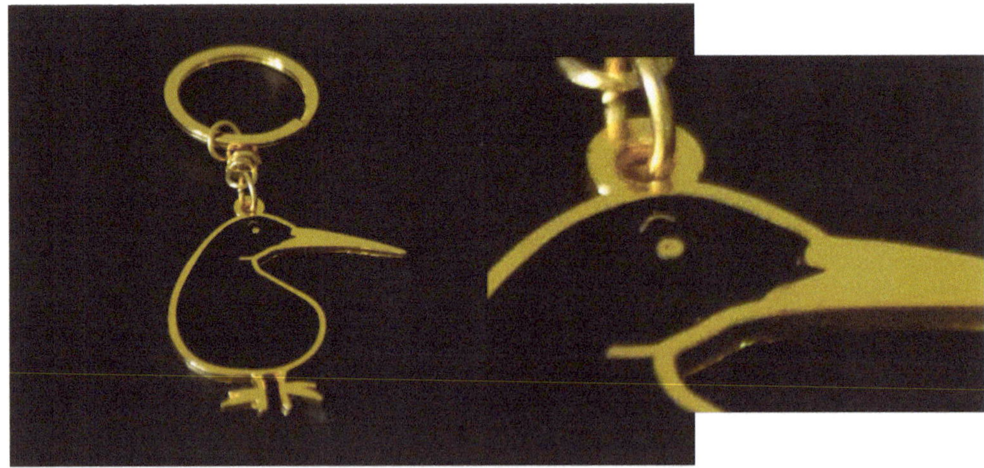

1600

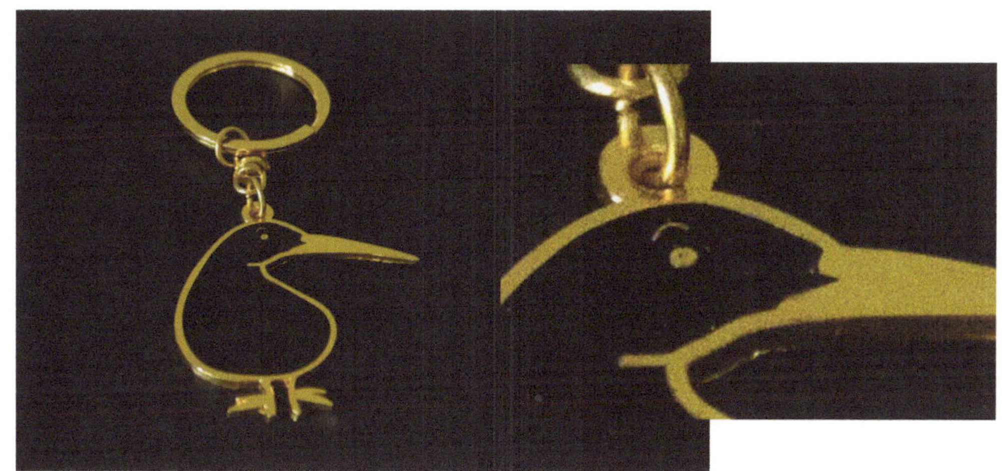

6400

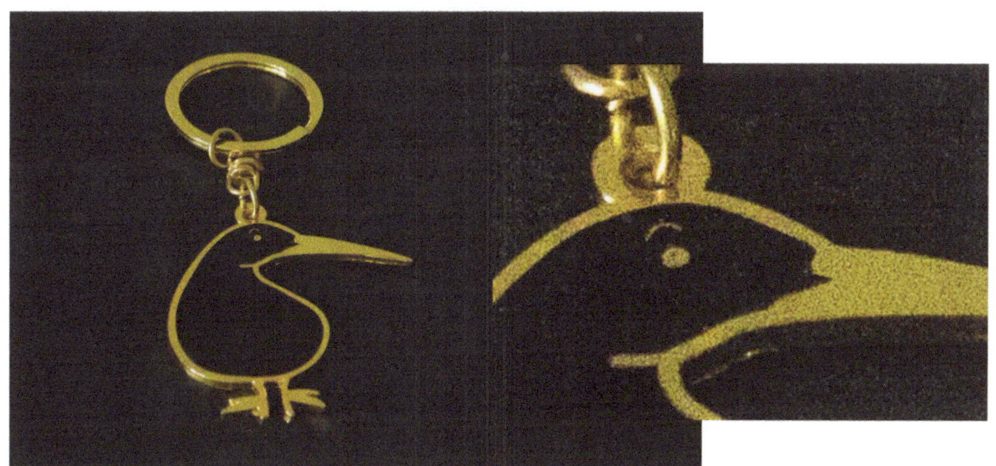

25600

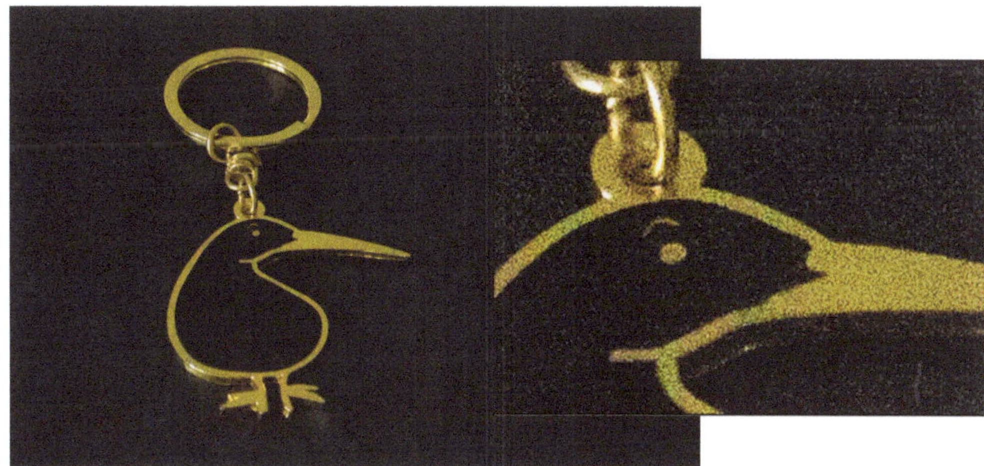

40000

When to Increase ISO

ISO is most commonly increased when:
- You are shooting in low light
- You need a faster shutter speed to freeze movement
- You want to avoid camera shake
- You cannot open the aperture any wider

In these situations, increasing ISO allows you to maintain the shutter speed and aperture you need.

ISO as the "Support Setting"

Many photographers think of ISO as a support setting, rather than the first choice.
A common approach is:
1. Choose a shutter speed based on movement
2. Choose an aperture based on depth of field
3. Adjust ISO to balance the exposure

This allows you to prioritise creative decisions first.

What to Take Away from This Chapter

- ISO controls how sensitive the camera is to light
- Increasing ISO makes images brighter
- Higher ISO can introduce noise, especially in darker areas
- Modern cameras handle high ISO better than ever
- ISO is often adjusted after shutter speed and aperture

In the next chapter, we'll bring everything together and look at how the Exposure Triangle works as a whole in real shooting situations.

How The Exposure Triangle Works Together

By now, you've seen how shutter speed, aperture, and ISO each affect exposure in different ways. The next step is understanding how they work together.

The Exposure Triangle is not about memorising settings. It's about understanding balance.

Each setting affects brightness, but each one also affects how your photo looks. This is why changing one setting usually means adjusting at least one of the others.

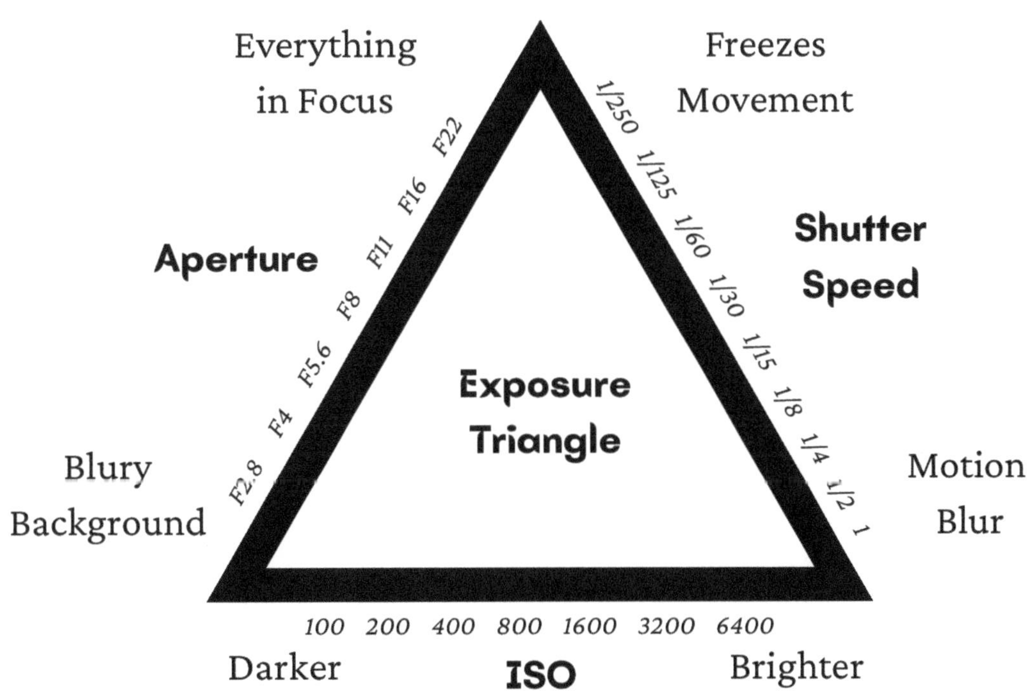

One Change Affects the Others

The three sides of the Exposure Triangle are linked.

If you change one setting, the amount of light captured by the camera changes. To keep the exposure balanced, you often need to compensate using another setting. A one-stop increase in one setting needs to be balanced by a one-stop decrease in another to maintain the same exposure.

For example:

- If you let in more light by opening the aperture, you may need to reduce how long light enters the camera by using a faster shutter speed
- If you allow light to enter the camera for longer using a slower shutter speed, you may need to reduce the amount of light entering the camera by using a smaller aperture
- If you increase ISO, you may need to reduce the shutter speed or use a smaller aperture to avoid overexposure.

These adjustments work together to control overall brightness.

Exposure Is a Series of Trade-Offs

Every exposure decision comes with a compromise.

When you adjust one setting to improve one aspect of your image, you often affect something else at the same time. A faster shutter speed might freeze movement, but it can reduce the amount of light reaching the sensor. A smaller aperture can increase depth of field, but it may require a slower shutter speed or higher ISO in lower light.

This is why exposure rarely feels like a simple on–off switch. Instead of searching for a perfect combination of settings, photographers are constantly weighing up which result matters most for the photo they're taking.

Understanding exposure means recognising these trade-offs and making deliberate choices. Every time you change a setting there will be both benefits and drawbacks. Once you understand this, exposure becomes much easier to manage and far less frustrating.

Same Exposure, Different Results

One of the most important things to understand is that there is more than one way to achieve a similar exposure.

Even when two images are exposed to the same overall brightness, the creative choices behind them can be very different. This is because shutter speed, aperture, and ISO each prioritise different aspects of a scene.

Two photos can look equally bright but feel very different because:
- One uses a fast shutter speed and freezes motion
- Another uses a wide aperture and blurs the background
- Another uses a higher ISO to allow a usable shutter speed in low light

This is why there is rarely a single "correct" exposure setting.

The images below show how different combinations of settings can produce a similar exposure, while creating a very different look.

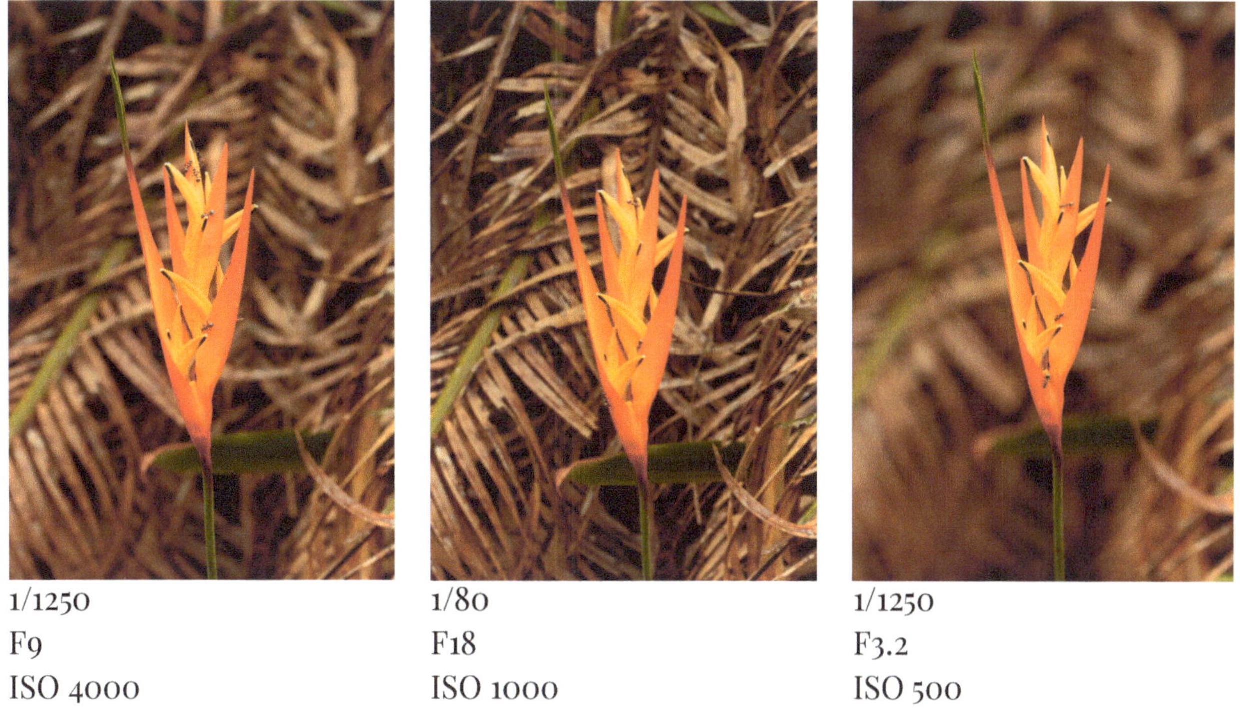

1/1250
F9
ISO 4000

1/80
F18
ISO 1000

1/1250
F3.2
ISO 500

Why Exposure Feels Like a Balancing Act

Exposure can feel tricky at first because every decision involves a trade-off.
- Shutter speed affects motion and camera shake
- Aperture affects depth of field
- ISO affects image quality

There is no way to change exposure without affecting something else, which is why exposure decisions often feel interconnected rather than isolated.

Choosing one setting often means accepting the side effects of another. Learning exposure is really about learning which trade-offs matter most for the photo you're taking.

Over time, these trade-offs become easier to recognise. Instead of thinking about numbers, you'll start to notice how changes affect the image itself — and adjust more instinctively.

You Don't Change Everything at Once

A common mistake is trying to adjust all three settings at the same time.

In practice, most photographers work the other way around:
1. Decide what matters most in the scene
2. Set the setting that controls that effect
3. Use the remaining settings to balance exposure

This approach simplifies decision-making and builds confidence.

Priority-Based Thinking

Here are some common priorities:
- If your subject is moving, shutter speed is usually the priority
- If depth of field matters most, aperture is usually the priority
- If light levels are low and other settings are limited, ISO is adjusted to support them

This way of thinking allows you to stay in control, even as light conditions change.

The Exposure Triangle Is a Guide, Not a Rule

The Exposure Triangle is a way of understanding how your camera behaves. It's not something you need to follow rigidly.

Sometimes the technically "correct" exposure doesn't match the look you want — and that's okay. Photography is subjective, and creative choices always come first.

As you practise, these decisions will start to feel more natural and less technical.

Later in the book we'll look more closely at how to decide which setting should take priority in different situations.

What to Take Away from This Chapter

- The three exposure settings are linked
- Changing one usually means adjusting another
- There are many ways to achieve a similar exposure
- The goal is balance, not perfection
- Prioritising what matters most simplifies exposure decisions

In the next chapter, we'll move from understanding exposure to using your cameras light meter to choose the right exposure settings.

Using The Light Meter

What the Light Meter Does

Your camera has a tool called a light meter that helps you judge exposure.

It measures the light in a scene and suggests whether your current settings will produce an image that the camera considers correctly exposed — not too bright and not too dark.

The key thing to remember is that the light meter is a guide, not a decision-maker. It doesn't know what you're photographing or how you want the image to look. It simply responds to the light it sees.

How the Light Meter Is Displayed

In most cameras, the light meter appears as a scale with a marker that moves left or right as you adjust your settings.

In most cameras, the light meter can be seen through the viewfinder and is also displayed somewhere on the rear LCD screen. Depending on your camera model, you may need to press the info or display button to make it visible. Once you know where to find it, the light meter becomes an easy reference that you can check quickly while adjusting your settings.

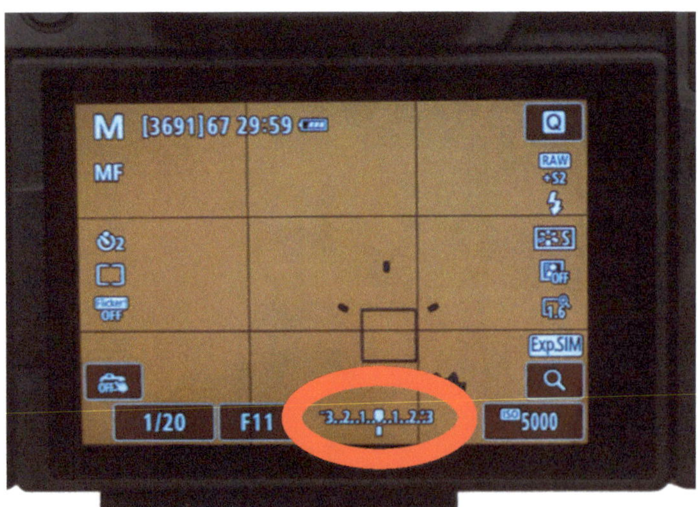

Depending on your camera the light meter maybe displayed in a different location or appear slightly different to what you can see in the image to the right.

The centre (0) indicates what the camera thinks is a balanced exposure.
Negative values (–) suggest underexposure, and positive values (+) suggest overexposure.

The numbers on either side represent full stops. For example, +1 means the image is one full stop overexposed, and +2 means it is two full stops overexposed. Likewise, –1 means one full stop underexposed, and –2 means two full stops underexposed.

The smaller marks or dots between the numbers represent third stops.

As you change shutter speed, aperture, or ISO, the meter moves to show how those changes affect exposure.

This visual feedback is what makes the light meter so useful — it allows you to see the effect of your adjustments in real time.

Correctly Exposed

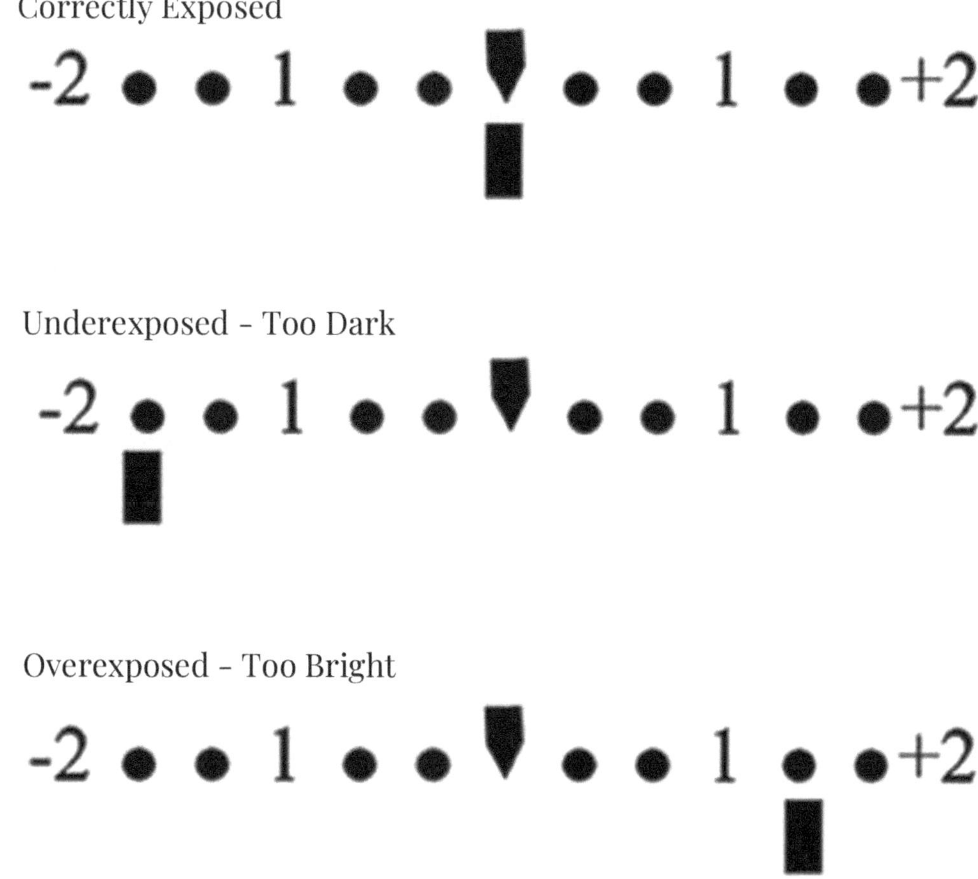

What the Light Meter Is Actually Aiming For

By default, your camera's light meter is trying to make everything it sees average out to a mid-tone.

This works well for many scenes, but it can struggle when the scene is dominated by:

- Bright tones (sand, water, sky)
- Dark tones (shadows, dark foliage, night scenes)
- Strong contrast between light and dark areas

In these situations, the light meter may suggest settings that don't match what your eyes are seeing — and that's where understanding becomes more important than obedience.

When the Light Meter Works Well

The light meter is most reliable when:

- Light is even and consistent
- The scene contains a mix of highlights, mid-tones, and shadows
- You're aiming for a natural-looking exposure

In these situations, using the light meter as a starting point can get you very close to a good exposure quickly.

This is why the light meter is especially helpful when you're learning — it gives you a reference point to work from.

On overcast, cloudy days the light meter is usually pretty accurate because the light is soft and there is not a great difference or contrast between the shadows and highlights.

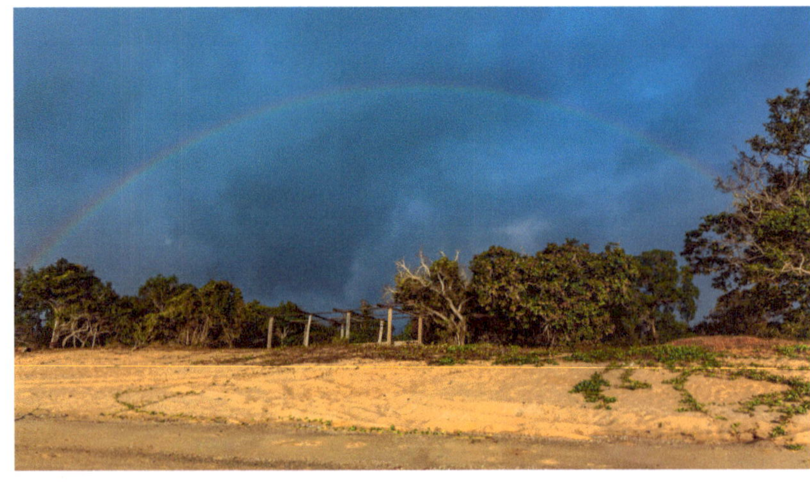

When the Light Meter Can Be Misleading

The light meter can struggle when the scene doesn't match its expectations.
For example:

- A bright beach scene may be underexposed because the camera tries to darken the brightness
- A dark rainforest scene may be overexposed because the camera tries to brighten the shadows
- Backlit subjects may appear too dark if the meter prioritises the bright background

In these cases, blindly following the meter can lead to results that don't reflect the scene as you experienced it.

Compose First, Then Check the Meter

One thing to remember about the light meter is that it is always measuring the light entering your lens. If you move the camera, the amount of light in the frame can change, and the meter reading will change as well.

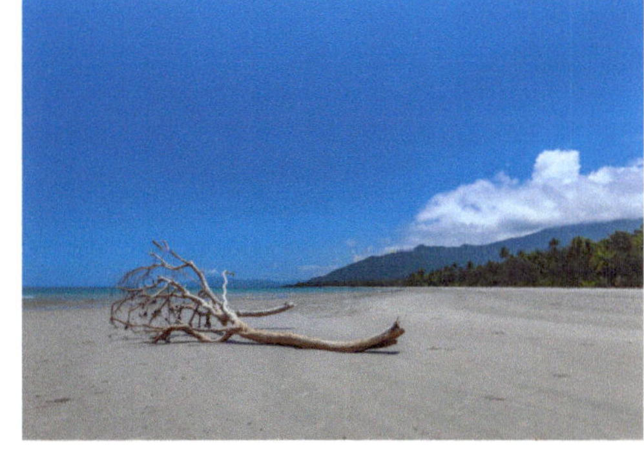

For this image I had to underexposure by 1 stop from what the light meter suggested to compensate for the bright sun and white sand.

For example, if you tilt the camera slightly upwards and include more bright sky, the meter may suggest that the image is overexposed. If you point the camera down towards darker areas, the meter may suggest the image is underexposed.

Because of this, it is important to compose your photo first, and then check the light meter.

A common mistake beginners make is setting their exposure before they have finished composing the image. When they then move the camera to frame the shot properly, the light meter changes and the exposure they set may no longer be correct.

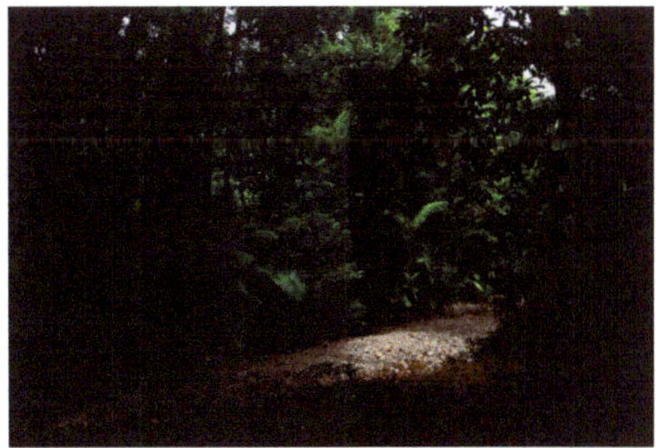

This image appears dark because the light meter exposed for the one spot of sun coming through the trees.

By composing your image first, the light meter reads the light from the exact scene you are photographing.

Using the Light Meter as a Starting Point

Rather than asking, "What does the light meter want?", a better question is: "Is this exposure doing what I want?"

A simple approach:
1. Set your exposure using the light meter as a guide
2. Take a photo
3. Review the result
4. Adjust if needed

This process builds confidence and helps you understand how your camera responds to different lighting situations.

Trusting the Meter vs Trusting Your Eyes

There will be times when you deliberately choose to ignore the light meter.

This might be because:
- You want a darker, moodier image
- You want to preserve highlights
- You want to emphasise silhouettes or shadows

Learning exposure isn't about always hitting zero on the meter. It's about recognising when the meter helps — and when your creative intent matters more.

What to Take Away from This Chapter

- The light meter measures light, not intention
- It aims for an average exposure, not a perfect one
- It works best as a guide and starting point
- Understanding when to override it builds confidence

In the next chapter, we'll look at the histogram — another tool that helps you evaluate exposure but after the photo is taken.

Understanding the Histogram

The histogram is another tool your camera provides to help you judge exposure. Unlike the light meter, which guides you before you take a photo, the histogram helps you evaluate exposure after the photo has been taken.

At first glance, the histogram can look confusing or overly technical. In reality, it is simply a visual way of showing how bright or dark your image is overall.

Once you understand what you're looking at, the histogram becomes one of the most reliable exposure tools available.

What a Histogram Shows

A histogram is a graph that represents the brightness values in an image.

- The left side of the graph represents dark tones and shadows
- The middle represents mid-tones
- The right side represents bright tones and highlights

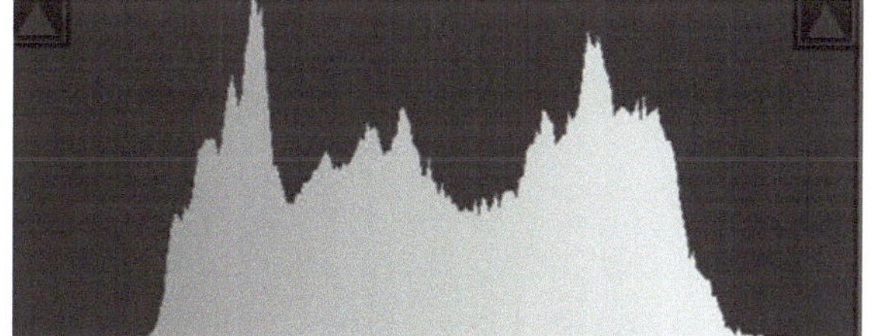

The height of the graph shows how much of the image falls into each brightness range. This means the histogram is not showing where things are in the image — it is showing how bright or dark the image is as a whole.

Where to Find the Histogram

The histogram is usually viewed after a photo has been taken.

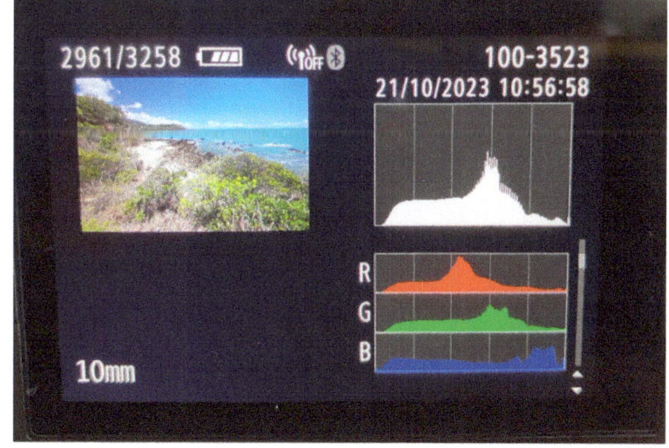

On most cameras, it can be found:

- In playback mode
- By pressing the info or display button
- Or by enabling it in the camera menu

Histograms can also be seen in editing software such as Adobe Lightroom, where they are often used to help fine-tune exposure during post-processing.

What the Histogram Is Helping You Check

The histogram is especially useful for showing things that can be hard to see on the camera's LCD screen, particularly in bright sunlight.

It helps you quickly check:
- Whether highlights are too bright
- Whether shadows are too dark
- Whether important detail may be lost

This makes the histogram a valuable tool for reviewing images in the field.

Overexposed and Underexposed Histograms

When most of the graph is pushed toward the right, the image is likely overexposed. Bright areas may have lost detail, especially if the graph is touching the right edge.

When most of the graph is pushed toward the left, the image is likely underexposed. Dark areas may lack detail, especially if the graph is touching the left edge.

It's important to pay attention to where the histogram is touching the edges of the graph. When the graph is pushed hard against the left or right side, it usually means that detail has been lost in those areas. This loss of detail cannot always be recovered later, even when editing. By checking the histogram and making small exposure adjustments, you can often prevent this and preserve important information in your image.

Correctly Exposed

Overexposed – Too Bright

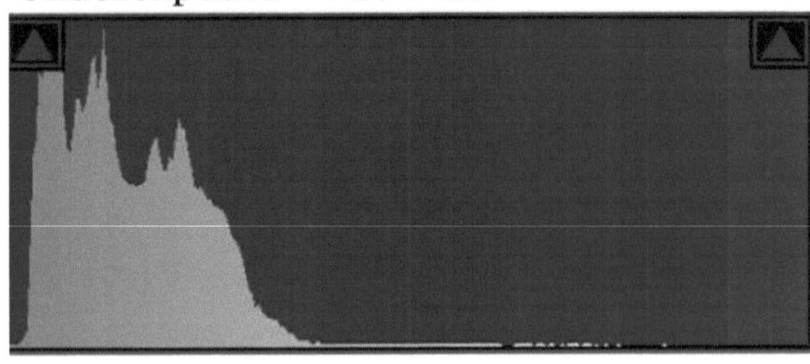

Underexposed – Too Dark

What a "Correct" Histogram Looks Like

One of the most important things to understand is that there is no single correct histogram shape.

A well-exposed image does not always have:

- A centred graph
- A smooth bell curve
- Even distribution across the chart

Instead, a correct histogram is one that suits the scene and retains detail where it matters.

Different Scenes, Different Histograms

Some scenes naturally produce histograms that lean to one side.

For example:

- A bright beach scene may produce a histogram weighted toward the right
- A dark rainforest scene may produce a histogram weighted toward the left
- A high-contrast scene may show peaks at both ends

These histograms can still represent a correct exposure, as long as important detail is not lost.

This is where understanding the scene is just as important as reading the graph.

Correctly Exposed

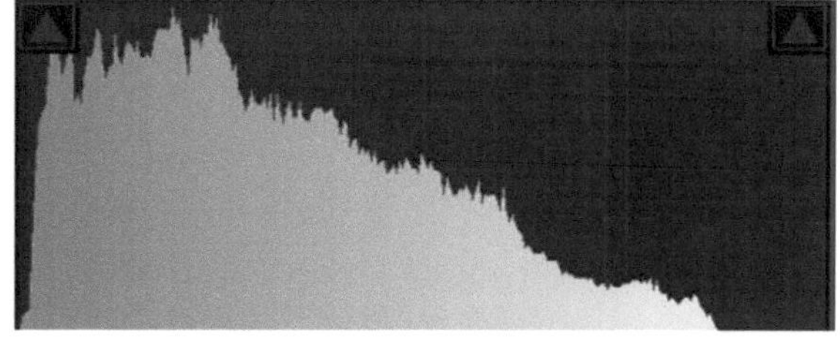

Correctly Exposed

Correctly Exposed

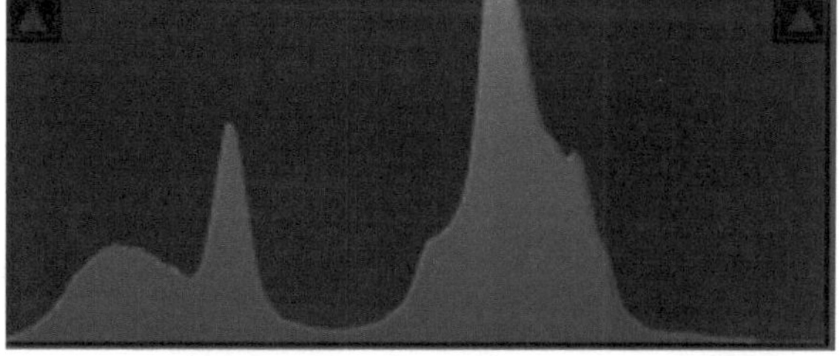

Correctly Exposed

Correctly Exposed

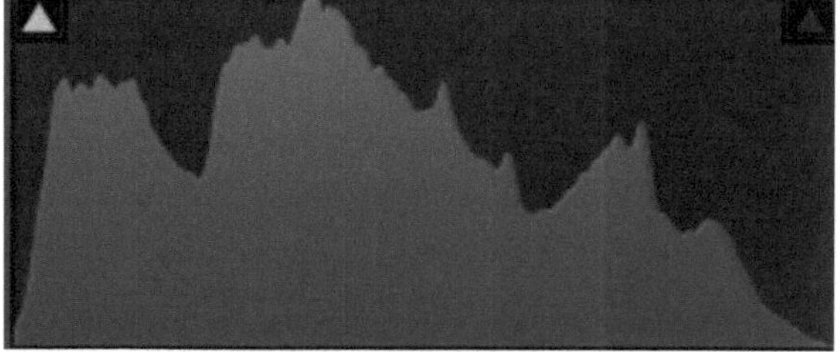

Colour Histograms (RGB)

Some cameras display a colour histogram, showing separate graphs for red, green, and blue.

These colour channels can help you spot exposure issues that may not be obvious in the overall histogram. For example, one colour channel may be pushed hard against the edge of the graph, meaning detail in that colour has become too bright or too dark and may no longer be visible in the image, even if the overall exposure looks acceptable.

This is particularly useful in scenes with strong colours, sunsets, or artificial lighting.

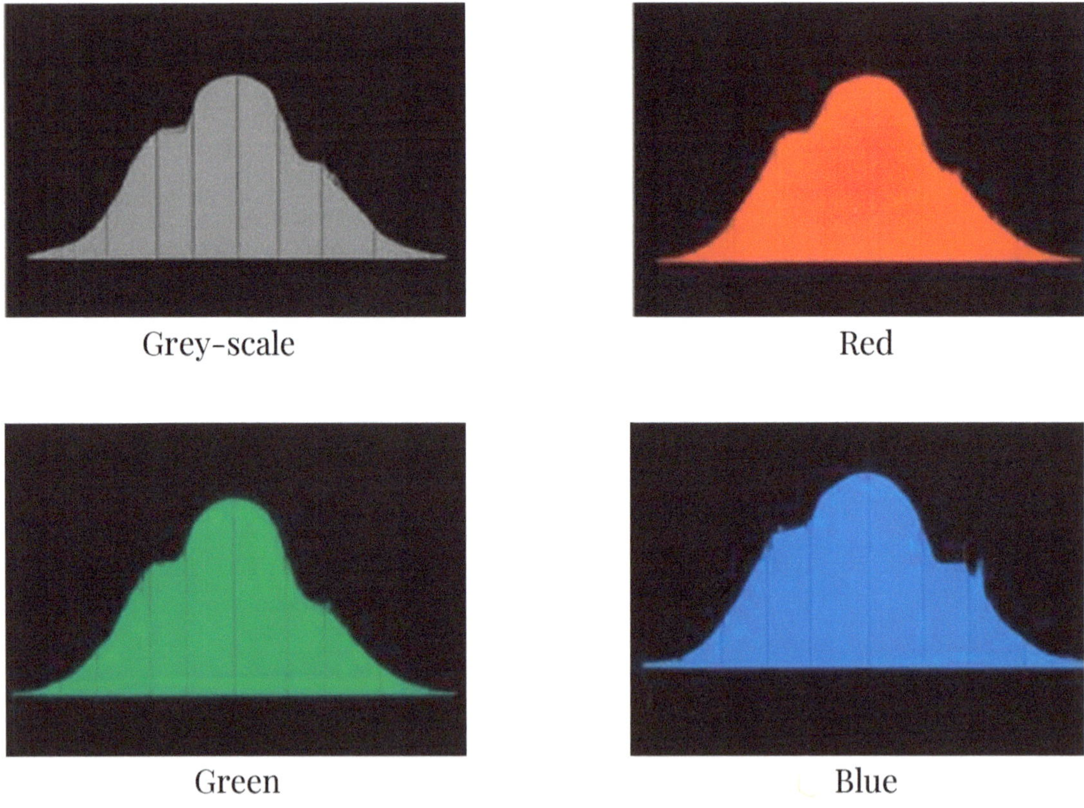

Grey-scale

Red

Green

Blue

On the next page are the images which I shared at the beginning of the book to show what exposure is, with a multicoloured histogram so you can see how the histogram changes as we go from very overexposed through correctly exposed to very underexposed. Pay attention to which colours move the most in the histogram and how those colours appear in the images.

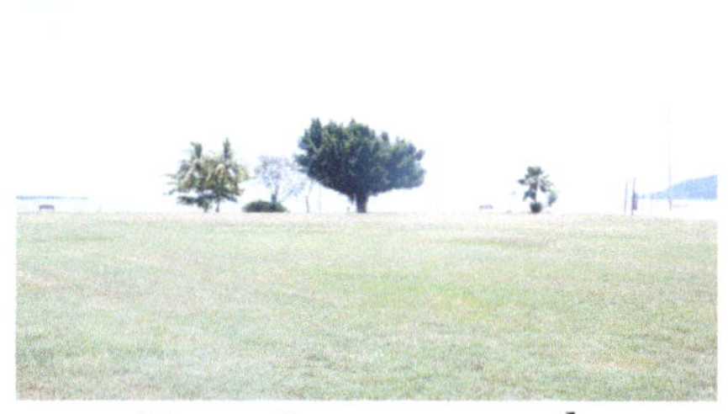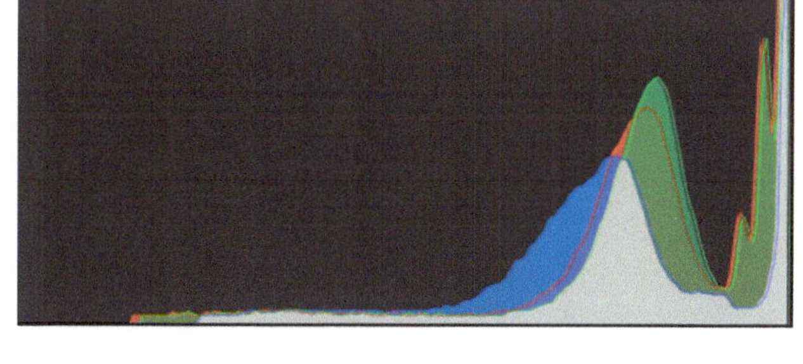

Very Overexposed

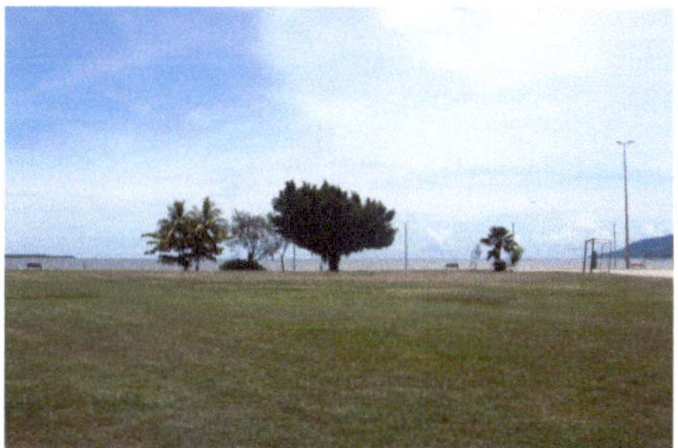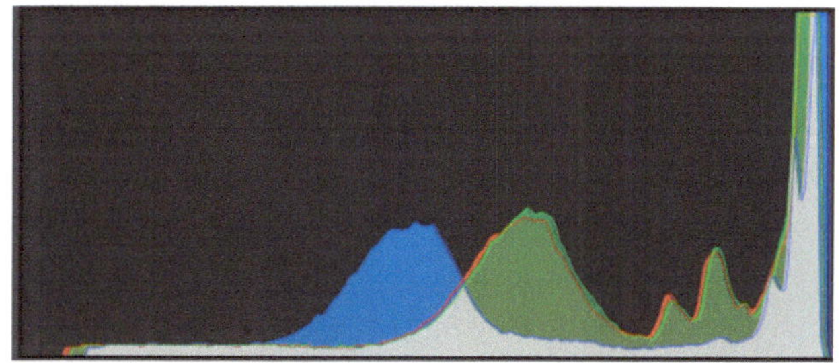

Overexposed

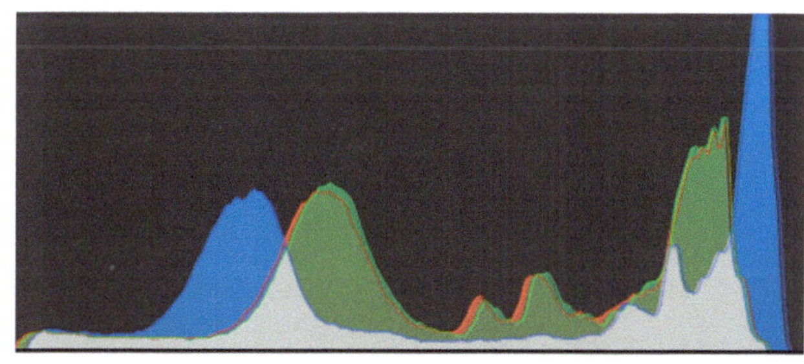

Correctly Exposed

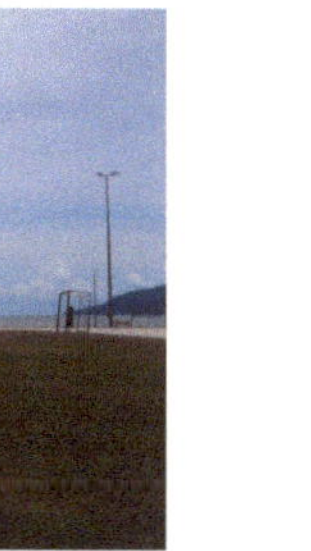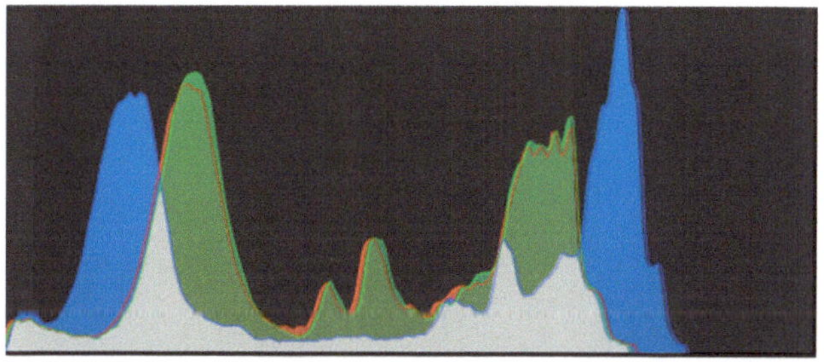

Underexposed

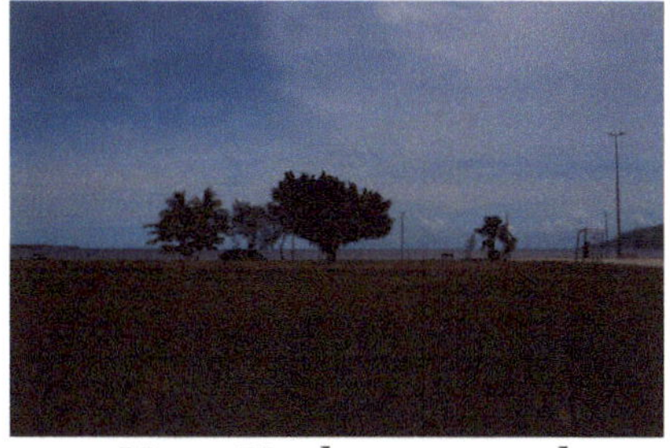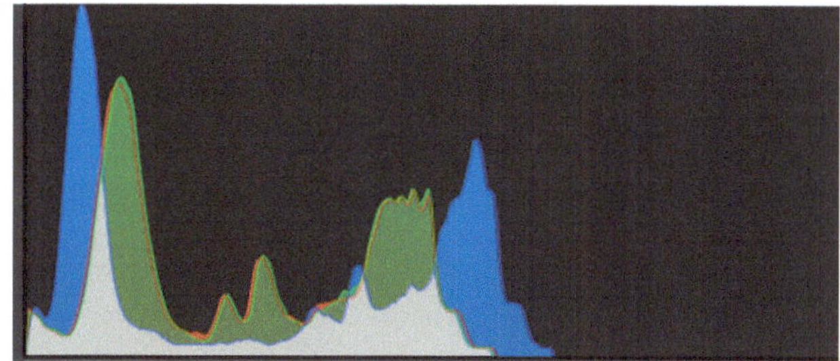

Very Underexposed

When the Histogram Matters Most

The histogram is especially helpful when:
- Shooting in bright sunlight
- Photographing high-contrast scenes
- Working quickly and needing confirmation
- Reviewing images on a small screen

It provides an objective reference when your eyes might be fooled by lighting conditions.

When to Trust Your Eyes Instead

Just like the light meter, the histogram is a guide — not a rule.

There will be times when:
- You intentionally create silhouettes
- You want deep shadows
- You allow highlights to blow out for creative effect

In these situations, the histogram may suggest an "incorrect" exposure, even though the image matches your intention.

Understanding the histogram gives you the confidence to choose when to follow it and when to ignore it.

Highlight Warnings and Clipping Alerts

Many cameras have an option to display highlight warnings, sometimes shown as flashing or blinking areas on the image during playback.

These warnings indicate areas of the photo that are so bright that detail may have been lost. This feature can usually be turned on in the camera's menu and is often referred to as highlight warnings or highlight alerts.

Used alongside the histogram, highlight warnings provide a quick and visual way to check whether important bright areas of your image have been overexposed. They are especially useful when shooting in bright conditions where it can be difficult to judge exposure on the camera's screen.

Like the histogram and light meter, highlight warnings are a guide. They help you make informed decisions, but they don't replace your creative intent.

What to Take Away from This Chapter

- The histogram shows how bright or dark your image is overall
- It helps identify lost detail in shadows and highlights
- There is no single correct histogram shape
- Different scenes produce different histograms
- The histogram is a guide, not a judgement

In the next chapter, we'll bring these tools together and look at choosing the right settings in real-world situations.

Choosing The Right Settings

By this point in the book, you've learned what shutter speed, aperture, and ISO do, and how they work together. The next step is learning how to decide which setting to adjust first.

When I'm choosing my exposure settings, I always start by asking myself two simple questions:
1. Is the subject moving?
2. How much of the image do I want to be in focus?

These two questions help me decide which setting to prioritise and in what order to make adjustments.

Question 1: Is the Subject Moving?

The first thing to consider is whether anything in the scene is moving — or whether there's a risk of camera shake.

If the subject is moving, or if I'm hand-holding the camera in low light, shutter speed is usually the most important setting to choose first. This ensures the movement is recorded the way I want it to be, whether that means freezing action or allowing blur.

If nothing is moving and the camera is well supported, shutter speed becomes less critical, giving more flexibility with the other settings.

Question 1: Is the subject moving?
 Yes — the bee is constantly moving, and even a light breeze can cause the flower to move, so a faster shutter speed is needed.

Question 2: How much of the image do I want in focus?
 Only the bee and the flower, which means using a wide aperture (low f-number) to keep the background soft and out of focus.

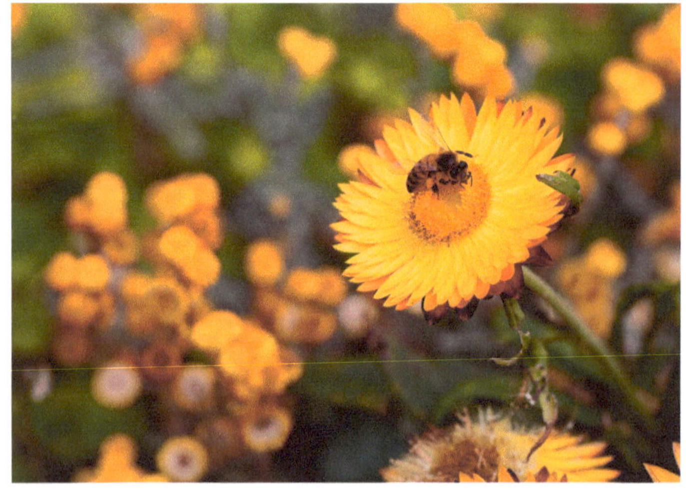

Question 2: How Much of the Image Do I Want in Focus?

Once I've thought about movement, the next question is depth of field.

If I want:

- A blurred background and strong subject separation, I choose a wide aperture
- Most or all of the scene in focus, I choose a smaller aperture

This decision has a big impact on the overall look of the image, which is why aperture is often chosen early in the process.

Choosing the Order of Your Settings

These two questions determine the order in which settings are chosen.

In many situations, the process looks like this:

1. Choose a shutter speed based on movement
2. Choose an aperture based on depth of field
3. Adjust ISO to balance the exposure

In other situations, the order may change — and that's okay. The goal isn't to follow a strict formula, but to make deliberate decisions instead of guessing.

Using the Flowchart as a Guide

The flowchart on the following page shows a simple decision-making process you can use when choosing exposure settings.

It's designed to:

- Reduce overwhelm
- Give you a clear starting point
- Help you decide what to change first

You don't need to follow it perfectly every time. As you practise, these decisions will start to happen more naturally, and the flowchart will become something you think through rather than something you actively refer to.

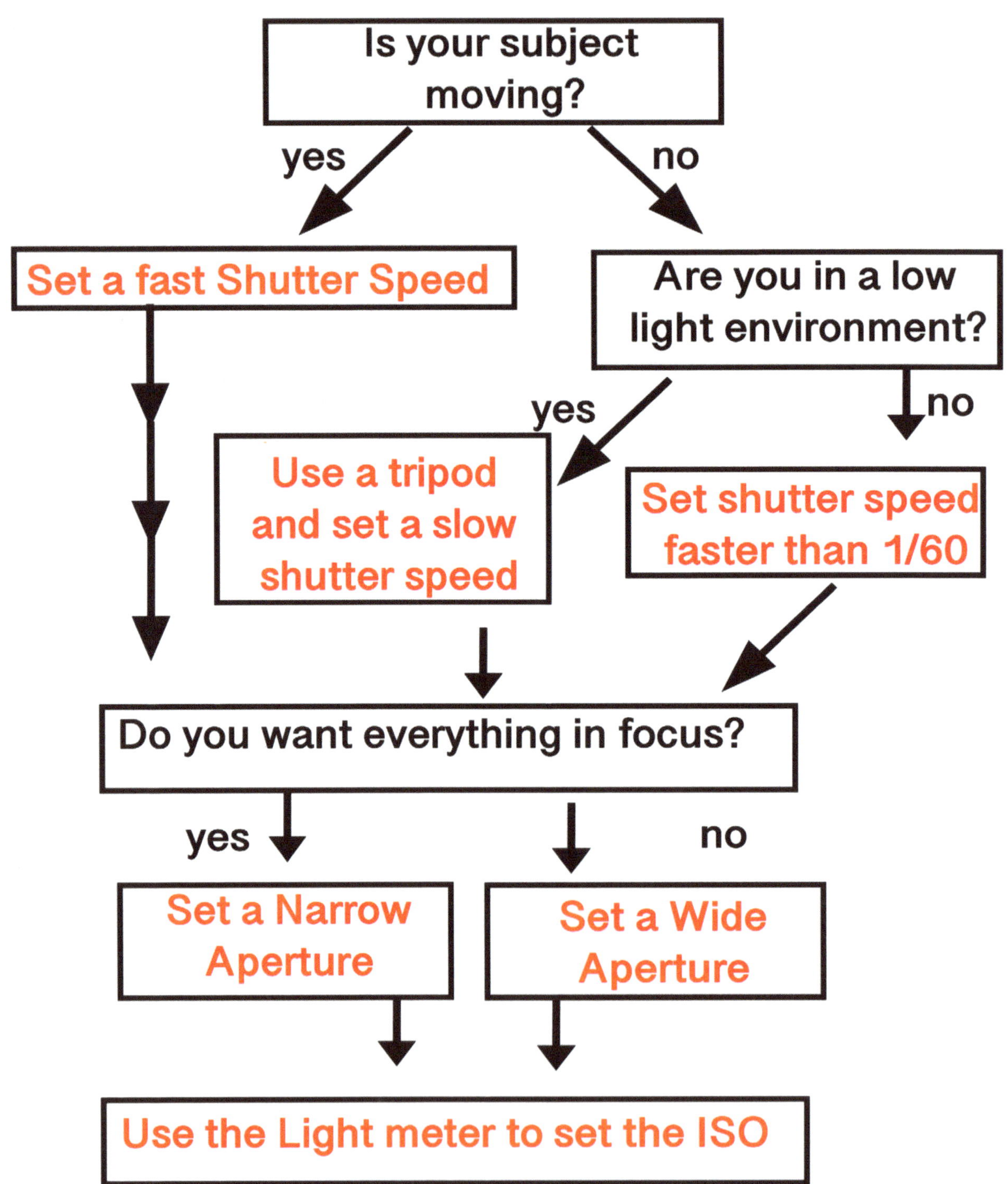

Is your subject moving?
yes
no
Set a fast Shutter Speed
Are you in a low light environment?
yes
no
Use a tripod and set a slow shutter speed
Set shutter speed faster than 1/60
Do you want everything in focus?
yes
no
Set a Narrow Aperture
Set a Wide Aperture
Use the Light meter to set the ISO

Adjusting ISO to Support Your Choices

Once shutter speed and aperture are set, ISO is usually adjusted last.

ISO is there to support the settings you've chosen for motion and depth of field. Increasing ISO allows you to maintain a faster shutter speed or a smaller aperture when light levels are low.

Because modern cameras handle ISO well, it's often better to increase ISO slightly than to sacrifice sharpness or the look you want.

Checking Your Exposure

After choosing your settings:
- Use the light meter as a guide
- Review the image on the screen
- Check the histogram

If the image isn't doing what you expected, make a small adjustment (one third stop) and try again. Exposure is rarely perfect on the first attempt, and that's completely normal.

What to Take Away from This Chapter

- Start with movement
- Then consider depth of field
- Choose settings in a logical order
- Use ISO to support your decisions
- Use your exposure tools as guides, not rules

Choosing the right settings becomes much easier once you have a clear way of thinking through the process.

In the next chapter, we'll look at controlling the light itself, and how changing the light around you can be just as powerful as changing your camera settings.

Controlling the Light Itself

Up to this point, we've focused on controlling exposure using the settings inside your camera — shutter speed, aperture, and ISO.

But there is another part of exposure that doesn't live in the camera at all.

Sometimes, the most effective way to change your exposure is to change the light itself.

Exposure Is Not Only a Camera Decision

When you're learning photography, it's easy to think that every exposure problem can be solved by adjusting a setting. In reality, many exposure challenges come from the lighting conditions rather than the camera.

If the light is harsh, flat, or uneven, no combination of settings will fully fix that. This is especially true when photographing outdoors, where light is constantly changing.

Understanding that you can influence the light — even in small ways — gives you more control and reduces frustration.

Working With Natural Light Outdoors

Most photographers work primarily with natural light, particularly when photographing landscapes, wildlife, or everyday scenes.

While you can't control the sun itself, you can control how you interact with it.

Small changes can make a big difference:
- Moving a few steps into shade
- Changing your shooting angle
- Turning your subject slightly
- Waiting for a cloud to soften the light

These choices often have more impact on the final image than changing a camera setting.

Timing Is a Form of Light Control

One of the most powerful ways to control light is simply choosing when to take the photo.

Light changes throughout the day:
- Early morning and late afternoon light is softer and warmer
- Midday light is often harsh and contrasty
- Overcast light can be even and gentle

Sometimes the best exposure decision is to wait — or to come back later when the light suits the scene better.

In the photo taken at 2pm, (middle of the day) we have a lot of contrast and very little detail. The same scene taken later in the day shows more colour and detail in the subjects.

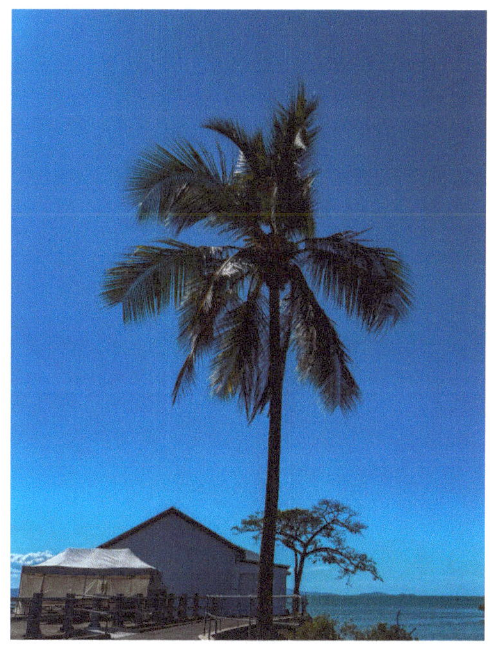

2pm

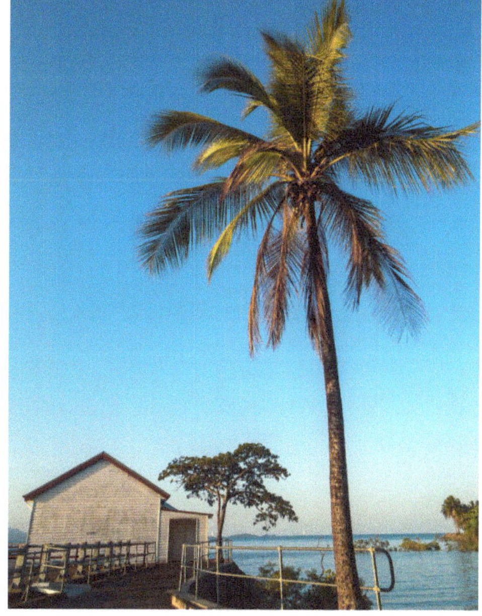

5pm,

Using the Environment to Shape Light

The environment around you can act as a natural lighting tool. Trees, buildings, rocks, and even your own body can be used to block light and create shade. By reducing the amount of direct light reaching your subject, you can lower contrast and soften harsh highlights, making the light more even and easier to work with.

Using these elements allows you to shape the light without any equipment, which is especially useful when working in natural settings.

Reflecting and Softening Light

Light doesn't only have to be blocked — it can also be redirected or softened.

A reflector is used to bounce light back onto a subject. A traditional reflector is usually a round or square piece of white or shiny material, often with a metallic surface similar to alfoil. Reflectors are commonly used in photography studios, but they work just as well outdoors by reflecting existing light back into shadow areas.

You don't need specialist equipment to use this idea. Light-coloured walls, sand, concrete, water, or even a white towel can all act as natural reflectors, helping to brighten shadows and reduce contrast.

A diffuser or scrim is used to soften light. It is usually made from a semi-transparent material and is placed between the light source and the subject. This spreads the light more evenly, reducing harsh shadows and bright highlights.

While diffusers and scrims are often used in studio photography, the same effect can be achieved on location. Thin fabrics, baking paper, or light sheets can all help soften direct sunlight, especially when photographing people, flowers, or small subjects outdoors.

This is a studio set up using both a difusser and a reflector. In this case the diffuser is a soft box placed over the light source, this softens the main light hitting the subject. The reflector is on the right and is reflecting the light from the softbox, making it even softer and lightening up the shadows gently.

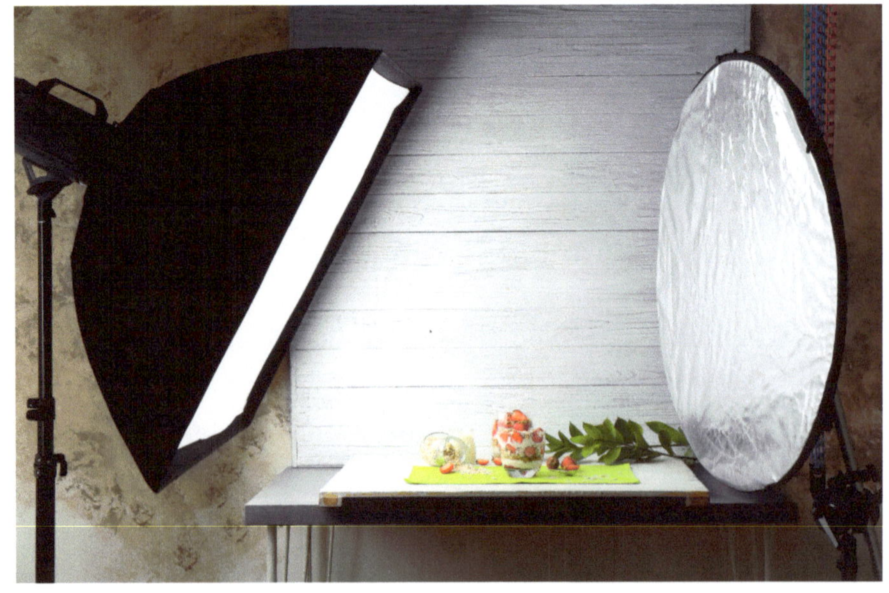

Adding Light When Needed

Another way to control light is to add your own.

Many cameras have a built-in flash, and some photographers also use an external flash mounted on the camera's hot shoe. Flash can be used to add light to a scene, lift shadows, or balance bright backgrounds.

Light doesn't have to come from a flash, though. Small LED lights, torches, or continuous lights can also be used to add light where it is needed. Indoors, something as simple as turning on or off lamps or ceiling lights can change the quality and direction of light enough to make exposure easier to manage.

At this stage, it's not important to know how to use these light sources — only that adding light is an option. Even a small amount of extra light can make a big difference.

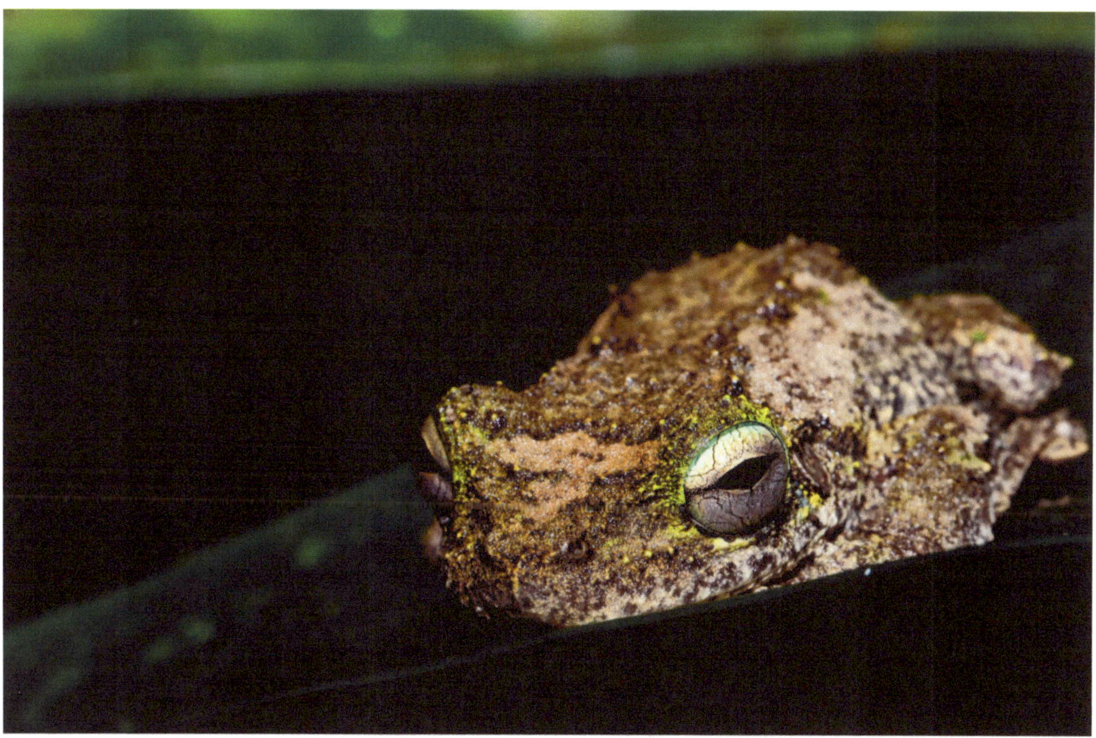

This image was taken at night. My Partner was holding a large torch light, shinning it at the frog. Without this extra light source it would have been very hard to get a properly exposed, clear image of the frog.

Choosing Light First, Then Settings

Once you start thinking about light itself, your approach to exposure often changes.

Instead of immediately adjusting settings, you may first:
- Change position
- Adjust timing
- Modify the light in the scene

Only then do you fine-tune your shutter speed, aperture, and ISO.

This approach often leads to more consistent and intentional results.

What to Take Away from This Chapter

- Exposure isn't controlled only by camera settings
- Light can be influenced, even outdoors
- Small changes in position or timing can have a big impact
- Sometimes changing the light is easier than changing settings

In the next chapter, we'll bring everything together and look at how all of these decisions work in real-world shooting situations.

Bringing It All Together

By now, you've learned what shutter speed, aperture, and ISO do, how they work together, and how tools like the light meter and histogram can help guide your decisions. You've also seen that exposure isn't only about camera settings — it's also influenced by the light around you.

This chapter is about stepping back and seeing how all of those pieces fit together in practice.

Exposure Is a Decision-Making Process

Choosing exposure settings is rarely about finding a perfect combination of numbers. It's about making a series of small decisions based on what you're photographing and what you want the image to look like.

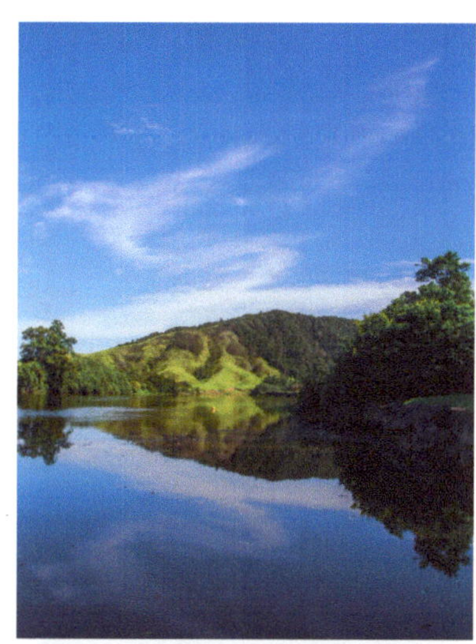

Most of the time, the process looks something like this:
- You observe the light
- You consider movement
- You decide how much of the scene should be in focus
- You choose settings in a logical order
- You review and adjust

This process becomes faster and more intuitive with practice.

Using Your Tools Together

The exposure tools in your camera are designed to support you, not to replace your judgement.
- The Exposure Triangle helps you understand how settings interact
- The light meter provides a starting point
- The histogram helps you review exposure after the photo is taken
- Highlight warnings can alert you to lost detail

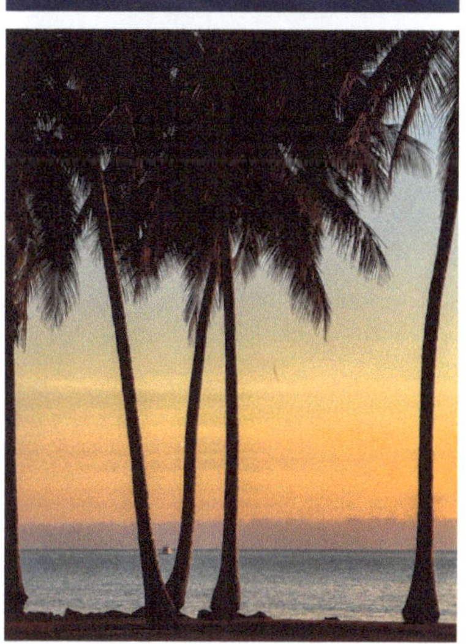

No single tool gives the full picture. Used together, they give you confidence and control.

There Is More Than One "Correct" Exposure

One of the most important things to remember is that there is rarely just one correct exposure.

Two photographers can photograph the same scene and make very different exposure choices and both images can be successful.

Exposure choices are influenced by; mood, subject, light and creative intent.

Learning exposure isn't about always getting it "right". It's about making intentional choices and understanding the results.

Trust Builds With Practice

At first, exposure decisions can feel slow and uncertain. That's completely normal.

Over time, you'll start to recognise patterns:
- When you need a faster shutter speed
- When depth of field matters most
- When to raise ISO without worrying
- When to trust your eyes over the light meter

The more you practise, the less you'll think about settings — and the more you'll focus on the image itself.

What to Take Away From This Chapter

- Exposure is a process, not a formula
- Camera settings, light, and tools all work together
- There is no single correct exposure for every scene
- Confidence comes from understanding and practice

In the next chapter, we'll look at camera modes and how they affect the way exposure decisions are made. Understanding these modes will help you choose the right level of control for different situations before moving on to the practical exercises later in the book.

Camera Modes

Most cameras offer several different shooting modes. These modes control how much decision-making the camera does for you, and how much control you have over your exposure settings.

Most photographers use Manual, Shutter Priority, and Aperture Priority. Understanding what each mode does will help you choose the right one for different situations.

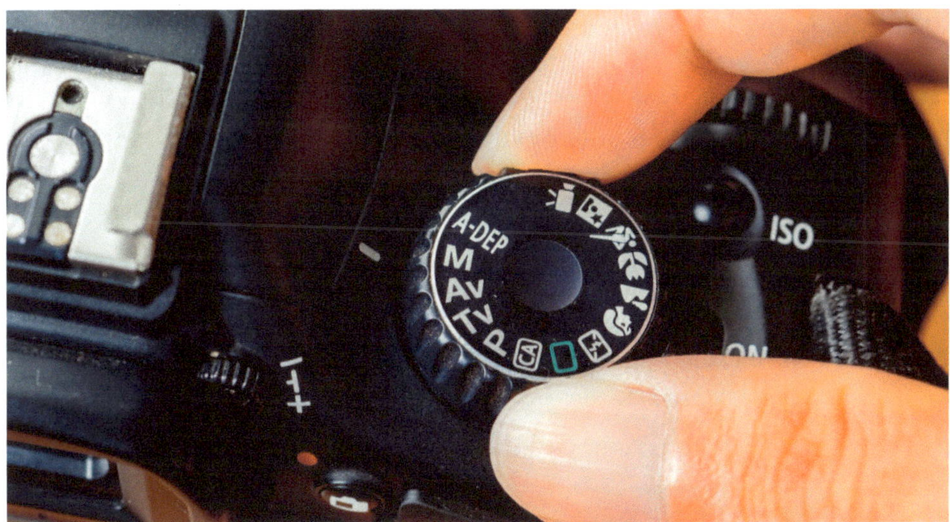

Auto Mode

In Auto mode, the camera makes all exposure decisions for you. It chooses the shutter speed, aperture, and ISO automatically.

This mode can be useful when you're just starting out or when you need to take a quick photo without thinking about settings. However, Auto mode gives you very little control over how the image looks, which makes it less useful when you're learning exposure.

Some people also find Auto mode useful as a learning tool. Taking a photo in Auto can give you an idea of the shutter speed, aperture, and ISO the camera chooses in a particular lighting situation. Reviewing these settings can be helpful when learning how exposure decisions are made.

Program Mode

Program mode is similar to Auto mode, but with slightly more flexibility. The camera still chooses the shutter speed and aperture, but you can adjust ISO.

Program mode can be a good stepping stone away from Auto, but it still doesn't give you full control over exposure decisions.

Shutter Priority Mode

In Shutter Priority mode, you choose the shutter speed, and the camera automatically selects an aperture to match. ISO can be left on auto or you can choose the ISO you want to use.

This mode is useful when movement is your main concern, such as:
- Freezing action
- Controlling motion blur
- Reducing camera shake when hand-holding the camera

Shutter Priority is especially helpful when photographing moving subjects or when you need to react quickly to changing situations.

Aperture Priority Mode

In Aperture Priority mode, you choose the aperture, and the camera automatically selects a shutter speed. ISO can be left on auto or you can choose the ISO you want to use.

This mode is useful when depth of field is your main priority, such as:
- Blurring the background
- Keeping more of the scene in focus
- Controlling how much separation there is between subject and background

Aperture Priority is commonly used for portraits, landscapes, and still-life photography.

Manual Mode

In Manual mode, you choose shutter speed, aperture, and ISO yourself.

This mode gives you the most control over exposure and is ideal when:
- The light is consistent
- You want predictable results
- You want to fully understand how exposure works

Manual mode may feel slower at first, but with practice it becomes very intuitive and is used throughout the exercises in this book.

Choosing the Right Mode

There is no single "best" camera mode.

Different modes are useful in different situations, and many photographers switch between them depending on what they are photographing. The important thing is understanding what each mode controls, so you can choose the one that suits your situation and your creative intent.

What to Take Away From This Chapter

- Camera modes control how exposure decisions are shared between you and the camera
- Shutter Priority and Aperture Priority are helpful learning tools
- Manual mode offers the most control and consistency
- Choosing a mode is about what you want to prioritise

In the next chapter, we'll look at how to change your camera settings and where to find the controls you'll need to use these modes in practice.

Changing Your Camera Settings

Every camera is a little different. Buttons, dials, and menus vary between brands and models, and even between cameras from the same manufacturer.

Rather than focusing on specific buttons, this chapter explains what to look for when changing your settings, so you can apply it to any camera you use.

On most modern cameras, each adjustment to shutter speed, aperture or ISO changes the exposure by one third of a stop.

Changing or Selecting Your Camera Mode

On many cameras, the mode dial is a physical dial on the top of the camera marked with letters such as A, S, P, and M. Turning this dial changes the camera mode. On some cameras, particularly smaller or more compact models, modes may be selected through the camera's menu system instead.

If your camera does not have a mode dial, look for a shooting mode option in the menu. Once selected, you can usually scroll through the available modes and confirm your choice.

Changing Shutter Speed

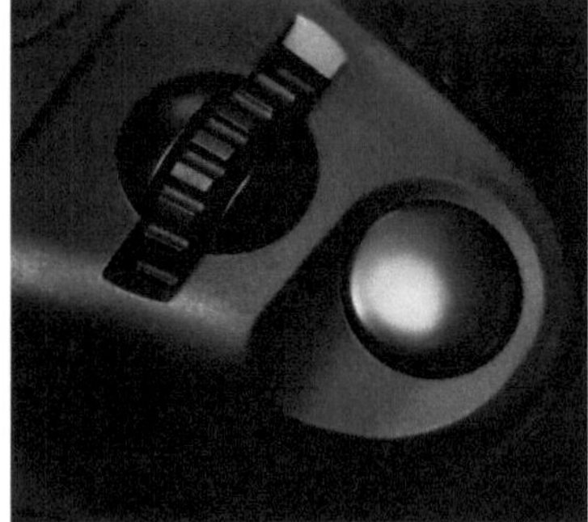

Shutter speed is usually adjusted using a dial on the camera body.

On many cameras, this is:
- A main dial near the shutter button, or
- A rear dial operated with your thumb

In Shutter Priority mode, adjusting this dial changes the shutter speed directly.
In Manual mode, the same dial is often used to change shutter speed, sometimes in combination with another button.

As you turn the dial, you will see the shutter speed change on the screen or in the viewfinder.

Changing Aperture

Aperture is commonly changed using:
- A second control dial, or
- The same dial used for shutter speed, combined with a button

In Aperture Priority mode, adjusting the dial changes the aperture directly.
In Manual mode, you may need to hold down a button while turning a dial.

You'll see the F-number update on the screen or in the viewfinder as you make changes.

Changing ISO

ISO is often changed by:
- Pressing a dedicated ISO button, or
- Accessing it through a quick menu or settings menu

Some cameras allow ISO to be assigned to a custom button or dial.

Once selected, you can usually adjust ISO using one of the control dials, just like shutter speed and aperture.

Using the Screen and Viewfinder

As you change settings, your camera will show you important information:
- Shutter speed
- Aperture
- ISO
- Light meter

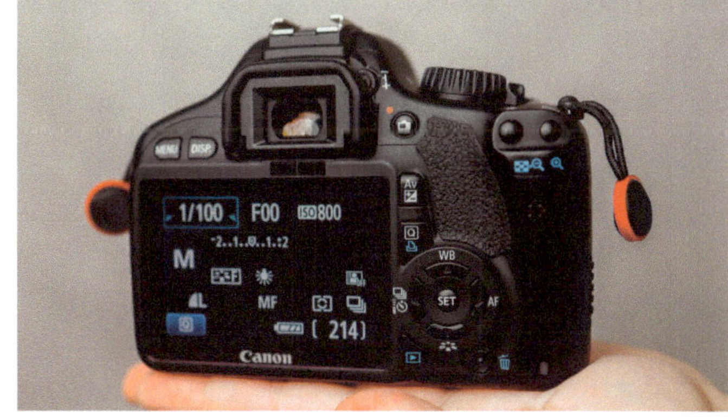

This information may appear:
- In the viewfinder
- On the rear LCD screen
- Or both

If you don't see this information straight away, look for an INFO or DISPLAY button to cycle through different display options.

Reviewing Your Settings After Taking a Photo

After taking a photo, you can review the settings used by viewing the image in playback mode. (look for a button with a play symbol to access playback mode)

Most cameras allow you to:
- Press the INFO or DISPLAY button while reviewing an image
- Cycle through screens showing shutter speed, aperture, ISO, histogram and other details

This can be a helpful way to learn, especially when comparing images taken with different settings.

Don't Worry About Getting It Perfect

You don't need to memorise where every button is straight away.

Learning your camera takes time, and it's normal to pause, check settings, and make adjustments as you go. The goal isn't speed — it's understanding.

As you work through the practice exercises, you'll naturally become more familiar with how to change settings on your camera.

What to Take Away From This Chapter

- Every camera is different, but the principles are the same
- Look for dials, buttons, and menus related to shutter speed, aperture, and ISO
- Use the screen and viewfinder to confirm your settings
- Reviewing settings after taking a photo is a valuable learning tool

In the next chapter, you'll put all of this into action with a series of practical exercises designed to build confidence with exposure.

Practice and Exercises

Understanding exposure is one thing. Feeling confident using it in real situations comes from practice.

The exercises in this chapter are designed to help you slow down, observe what's happening, and make deliberate exposure choices. There are no right or wrong results — the goal is to notice how changes to shutter speed, aperture, ISO, and light affect your images.

Before starting, find a still subject you can photograph repeatedly, such as an object on a table, a plant, or something outdoors that isn't moving. For the first few exercises, it's important that the light stays as consistent as possible, so try to avoid changing lighting conditions while you work through them.

It's best to complete these exercises in the order they are written, as they follow the structure of the book and build on each other. Working through them in sequence will help you see clearly how each part of the exposure triangle affects light and how the settings work together.

You don't need to complete all of the exercises at once. However, working through the first six exercises in one session can be especially helpful for developing a strong understanding of the exposure triangle. If something doesn't quite click the first time, revisit the exercise later — repeating even one exercise can be incredibly valuable.

As you practise, you may find it helpful to flip back through the book and revisit earlier sections. Concepts that felt unclear at first often make more sense once you've started applying them.

Make use of the tools built into your camera, such as the light meter, histogram, and highlight warnings. Notice how they respond as you change your settings, and how they help you assess whether an image is underexposed, overexposed, or balanced. Using these tools alongside your own judgement will help reinforce what you've learned and build confidence in evaluating exposure.

These exercises will help you put the ideas from this book into practice. The more you practise, the more natural these decisions will become — and before long, adjusting exposure will feel like second nature.

Exercise 1: Shutter Speed and Exposure

Put your camera on a tripod or stable surface (such as a table) so it cannot move.

Set your camera to Manual mode. Choose a still subject and keep the camera pointed at the same scene for the entire exercise.

Set your aperture to a mid-range value, such as F8, and set your ISO to a low value, such as ISO 100. These settings should stay the same for every image in this exercise.

Start with a shutter speed of 1 second and take a photo.
Increase your shutter speed a couple of stops at a time (for example, 1/2, 1/8, 1/25, and so on) until you reach 1/500 or faster, taking a photo at each step.

As you review the images, notice how the brightness of the image changes as the shutter speed increases. This exercise is designed to show how shutter speed controls the amount of light reaching the camera's sensor.

Exercise 2: Aperture and Exposure

Using the same subject and setup as Exercise 1, keep your camera on a tripod or stable surface (such as a table).

Set your camera to Manual mode.
Set your shutter speed to a mid-range value, such as 1/100, and set your ISO to a low value, such as ISO 100. These settings should stay the same for every image in this exercise.

Set your aperture to its widest setting (a low F-number) and take a photo.
Gradually make the aperture smaller a couple of stops at a time until you reach your smallest aperture (a high F-number), taking a photo at each step.

As you review the images, notice how the brightness of the image changes as the aperture changes. This exercise is designed to show how aperture controls the amount of light entering the camera.

Exercise 3: ISO, Exposure, and Noise

Using the same subject and setup as Exercise 1, keep your camera on a tripod or stable surface (such as a table).

Set your camera to Manual mode.
Set your shutter speed to a fast value, such as 1/500, and set your aperture to a small value, such as F16. These settings should stay the same for every image in this exercise.

Start with your lowest ISO and take a photo.
Increase the ISO a couple of stops at a time until you reach your highest ISO, taking a photo at each step.

As you review the images, notice how the brightness of the image changes, and pay attention to how noise becomes more visible as ISO increases. This exercise shows how ISO affects both exposure and image quality.

Exercise 4: Shutter Speed and Camera Shake

Remove the camera from the tripod and hand-hold it.

Set your camera to Shutter Priority mode and leave your ISO on a low value, such as ISO 100. Leave your lens at its widest focal length (zoomed out).

Start with a fast shutter speed 1/200 and take a photo of a still subject.
Gradually slow the shutter speed down, taking a photo at each step, until you reach 1/4

As you review the images, notice when camera shake begins to appear. This exercise helps you understand how slow is too slow when hand-holding the camera.

Exercise 5: Camera Shake and Focal Length

Repeat Exercise 4, but this time zoom in to a longer focal length. (or change to a lens with a longer focal length)

Set your camera to Shutter Priority mode and leave your ISO on a low value, such as ISO 100.

Start with a fast shutter speed 1/200 and take a photo of a still subject.
Gradually slow the shutter speed down, taking a photo at each step, until you reach 1/4

Compare the results to Exercise 4. As you compare these images, pay attention to how much more sensitive the camera becomes to movement when using a longer focal length. This is why faster shutter speeds are often needed when zooming in, even when photographing still subjects.

Exercise 6: Aperture and Depth of Field

Set up three still objects in a line, each at a different distance from the camera.

Set your camera to Aperture Priority mode. Set your ISO to 100 and keep it the same for every image.

Start with a wide aperture (a low F-number) and take a photo.
Gradually use smaller apertures (higher F-numbers), taking a photo at each step.

As you review the images, notice how depth of field changes, and how more or less of the scene appears in focus as the aperture changes. Look closely at which objects appear sharp and which fall out of focus as the aperture changes. Notice how depth of field is affected not just by aperture, but also by how close each object is to the camera. (You can learn more about this in my Focus Book)

Exercise 7: Shutter Speed and Motion

Put your camera in Shutter Priority mode.

Repeat Exercise 1, but this time photograph a moving subject, such as flowing water, waves, or traffic. (This works best when you have a subject or series of subjects moving at the same speed)

Keep your camera on a tripod or stable surface (such as a table), and keep your ISO the same throughout the exercise.

Start with a shutter speed of 1 second and gradually increase it a couple of stops at a time until you reach 1/500 or faster, taking a photo at each step.

As you review the images, notice how the appearance of movement changes — from smooth motion blur at slower shutter speeds to frozen detail at faster shutter speeds. This exercise shows how shutter speed affects the way movement appears in your photos.

Exercise 8: Movement and Decision-Making

Put your camera in Manual Mode.

Take your camera for a walk and look for moving subjects at different speeds.

Examples include:
- Trees moving in the wind
- People walking or running
- Cars
- Animals
- Flowing water

Use the flowchart in the book (page 56) to decide which settings to choose. Focus on asking yourself:
- Is the subject moving?
- How much of the image do I want in focus?

This exercise brings together shutter speed, aperture, and ISO in real situations.

Exercise 9: Changing Light

Put your camera in Manual Mode.

Photograph a sunrise, sunset or another scene where the light is changing quickly.

As the light changes, adjust your settings to maintain a correct exposure. Pay attention to how often you need to make changes and which settings you adjust first.

This exercise helps you practise responding to rapidly changing light, which is one of the most challenging — and rewarding — exposure situations.

Exercise 10: Same Scene, Different Settings

Choose a single scene with steady, consistent light. This could be an outdoor scene on an overcast day or an indoor scene with stable lighting.

Set your camera to Manual mode and aim to achieve a correct exposure.

Take three photos of the same scene, each time using a different combination of shutter speed, aperture, and ISO, while keeping the overall brightness of the image as similar as possible.

For example:
- One image might prioritise a fast shutter speed
- Another might prioritise a wide or narrow aperture
- Another might use a higher ISO to support the other settings

As you review the images, compare how they look and feel. Notice how motion, depth of field, and image quality change, even though the exposure is similar.

This exercise reinforces that there is more than one way to achieve a correct exposure, and that exposure choices are also creative choices.

Index

Learn More About Photography

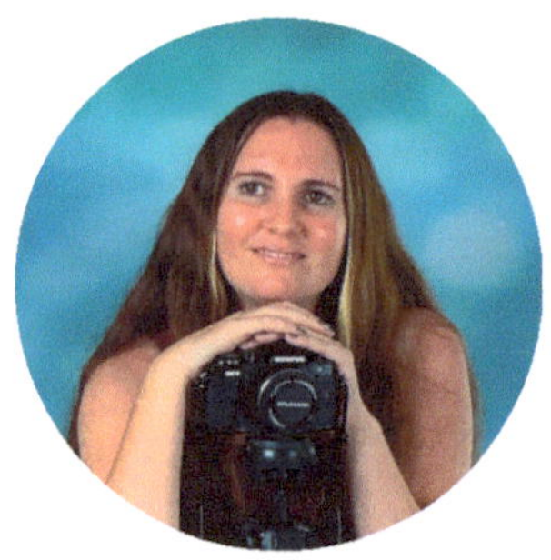

Hi, I am Tracey, I have been doing photography for nearly 20 years. I absolutely love photography and want to share that passion with other people. Sharing my knowledge of this creative world fills me with pride and accomplishment, especially when I see my students have a light bulb moment and everything finally makes sense for them. Having students excited to show me their work because they are happy with the result makes everything worth while.

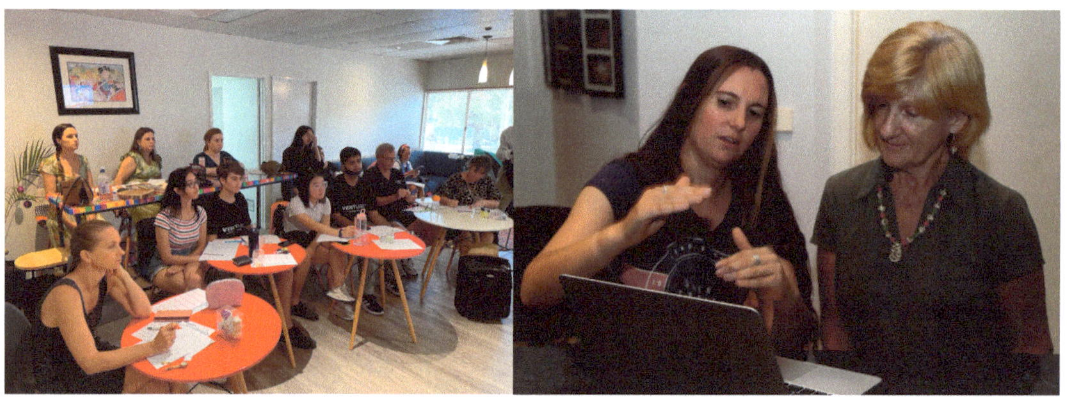

Whilst this book has given you an overview of the Exposure Triangle, this is only one part of photography. The photographic world is massive and you can keep learning new skills and techniques forever. This may seem daunting but I am here to help. I have a variety of online courses, in person courses, workshops, tours, E-book and PDF downloads available to be purchased from my website. No matter what option you choose I will always be there to answer your questions, provide inspiration and encourage you to try something new.

To continue your photography journey scan the QR code below!

traceyjonesphotography.com